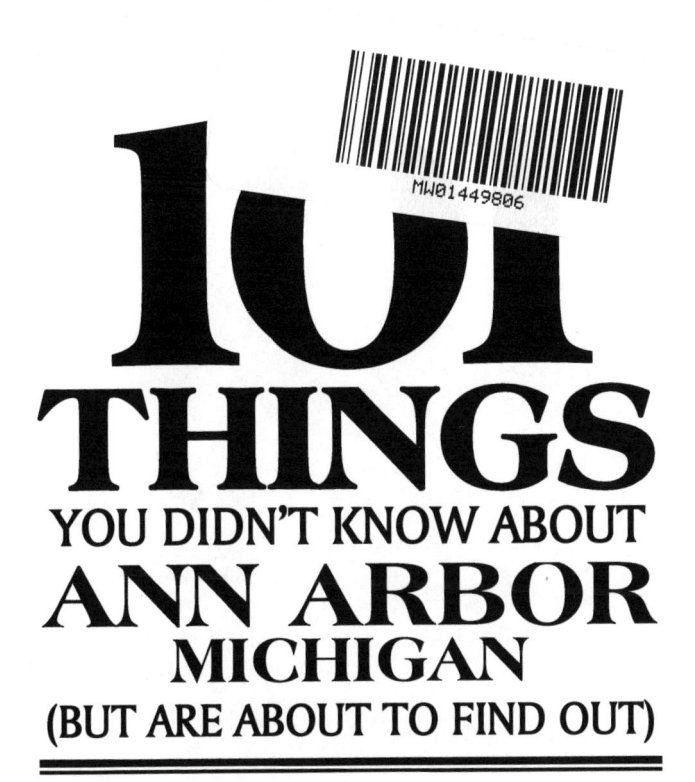

101 THINGS
YOU DIDN'T KNOW ABOUT
ANN ARBOR
MICHIGAN
(BUT ARE ABOUT TO FIND OUT)

By
Horace Martin Woodhouse

COPYRIGHT NOTICE

101Things You Things You Didn't Know About Ann Arbor, Michigan (But Are About to Find Out)
is published and copyrighted © 2010 by Curiosity Company (www.curiositycompany.com). All rights reserved. No part of this book may be reproduced in any form by any electronic or mechanical means (including photocopying, recording, or information storage or retrieval) without permission in writing from the publisher. Users are not permitted to mount any part of this book on the World Wide Web..

Direct-from-Publisher discounts are available for educators wanting to use our books in the classroom, and for charitable organizations wishing to sell Curiosity Company books for fundraisers.

For more information, go to:
www.curiositycompany.com

Printed in the United States of America.

Dedication

To the John and Jane Smiths of Ann Arbor

(It is said that each person to whom a book is dedicated, always buys a copy. If it proves true in this instance, good fortune is about to smile upon THE AUTHOR.)

INTRODUCTION

Awareness of the past is an important element in the love of place.
— Yi-Fu Tuan

After you've browsed through this little book, you will better understand why A^2 has a greater "quirk" quotient than most places. To prove his point, your curious author has dug up bits of esoterica — odd, amusing, and little-known strands that make up the city's variegated fabric.

Sure, you live here, but how much do you really know about Ann Arbor? Can you name your hometown football legends, *Playboy Magazine* playmates, 1960s radicals, NASA astronauts, the local boxer who fought Jack Dempsey, the brainy U-M graduate who attempted the "perfect crime," or the local girl who flirted with Humphrey Bogart in *The Big Sleep*? Who was the native industrialist who helped build the Panama Canal? Or the Ann Arborite who created the world's largest technology company? How did a border dispute lead to the greatest rivalry in college football? Where is the city's only Frank Lloyd Wright-designed house? What is Ann Arbor's connection a Presidential assassination? Readers learn the answers to these intriguing questions and much, much more.

Fascinating tangents and tidbits in purposely random sequence (with generous cross-references) create a ready-to-explore trail of knowledge about Ann Arbor and its environs, informing and entertaining, correcting myths and misconceptions, mostly revealing an unexpected treasure trove that brings a culture and a place into sharp focus.

1. Refuge of Scoundrels

The founders of Ann Arbor were two ne'er-do-wells named John Allen and Elisha Rumsey.

In the fall of 1823, with his family's Virginia property in foreclosure, Allen was trusted by several of his neighbors to drive their cattle to the Baltimore market and return with the proceeds. He completed the sale but pocketed the proceeds for himself. To avoid prosecution, he was forced to flee and abandon his family, heading to the unsettled West with hopes of making money in land speculation. He made his way to Buffalo, New York, and through Canada to Detroit, where he met Elisha Rumsey, who was on the run from a charge of embezzlement in New York.

The two men followed Indian trails along the Huron River to a spot where a creek would furnish power for saw and flour mills. On February 14, they returned to Detroit to register claims at the federal land office, using their ill-gotten funds. Allen purchased 480 acres for $600 and Rumsey purchased 160 acres of land for $200. They designated their settlement "Annarbour," inspired by Allen's wife, Ann (who would join him a year later) and for the surrounding stands of burr oak trees.

Allen established a post office in 1825, and became postmaster. He served as Coroner and Justice of the Peace and later won a seat in the State Senate. Rumsey built the town's first hotel and café.

2. Trapped in Cubicles

One of the world's leading manufacturers of office furniture and furniture systems, Herman Miller was founded by D. J. De Pree upon purchase of the Michigan Star Furniture Company in 1923 and named for his father-in-law, Herman Miller, an investor in the company. Company headquarters in the western Michigan town of Zeeland was settled primarily by Dutch immigrants, many of whom were skilled in the crafting of fine furniture.

During the 1960s, De Pree's son Hugh took over company management, and Herman Miller set out to change the configuration of the American office floorplan. The "Action Office System," created by a newly formed research team, headquartered in Ann Arbor and headed by inventor and sculptor Robert Propst, found that an open plan system broke up the monotony of previous plans and provided an illusion of privacy for each employee while also allowing proximity for easy communication with co-workers. It was the first open plan panel system in the world and subsequently fostered a multi-billion-dollar industry. The idea – now known simply as the office cubicle – transformed the way millions of people around the world do their daily business.

One aspect of the Action Office system that didn't take hold was the idea of doing office work in a standing position.

3. Pass the Salt

Born in Canada in 1872 to Scottish parents, David Murray Cowie journeyed to Michigan in 1892 to attend Battle Creek College, then transferred to the University of Michigan, where he graduated from the medical school and was hired as an assistant in internal medicine in 1896. He later earned a second medical degree at the University of Heidelberg in 1908.

When Cowie returned from Germany, he was recruited by medical dean George Dock to start a pediatrics department at the University of Michigan hospital. At the time, many children in the Great Lakes region suffered from goiters – swollen thyroid glands in the neck – due to a lack of iodine in the region's soil. At Cowie's suggestion, a state commission was appointed in 1922 to study the iodine deficiency problem. Cowie chaired the group, which first considered adding iodine to drinking water. When that proved too expensive, they switched to the idea of adding it to table salt. At their urging, iodized salt was marketed in Michigan beginning in 1924.

Before Cowie began his crusade, 35 percent of Michigan school children suffered from goiters. With the introduction of iodized salt, the incidence was reduced to 1.4 percent. The use of iodized salt spread throughout the country and eventually became commonplace in much of the world.

4. The Appointed One

Leslie Lynch King, Sr. was born in Chadron, Nebraska, the son of businessman Charles Henry King and Martha Alicia (Porter) King. He met and courted Dorothy Ayer Gardner, and they were married on September 7, 1912. A son, Leslie Lynch King, Jr., was born on July 14, 1913.

Sixteen days after the birth, Dorothy left the abusive marriage along with her son and moved in with her parents in Grand Rapids, Michigan. On December 19, 1913, an Omaha court granted a divorce to the Kings.

On February 1, 1917, Dorothy married businessman Gerald Rudolff Ford. They called her son Gerald Ford, Jr., although he was not formally adopted. In honor of his stepfather, young Gerald legally changed his name in 1935 to Gerald Rudolph Ford.

Attending the University of Michigan as an undergraduate, Ford played center and linebacker for the school's football team and helped the Wolverines to undefeated seasons and national titles in 1932 and 1933.

After serving nearly 25 years as Representative from Michigan's 5th congressional district, Ford became the first person appointed to the vice-presidency under the terms of the 25th Amendment. He ascended to the presidency upon Richard Nixon's resignation on August 9, 1974, the only chief executive who was elected neither President nor Vice-President.

5. Soap Opera

Born in Ann Arbor on November 19, 1972, Nicole Theresa Schmidt attended Adlai E. Stevenson High School in Livonia (also the alma mater of porn star Dani Woodward), where she took her first dramatic bow in a production of *The Sound of Music*. She spent a year studying musical theater at Western Michigan University before packing her bags to finish her degree at the American Academy of Dramatic Arts in Los Angeles. After graduation, she changed her surname to Forester (her paternal grandmother's maiden name) and began making the rounds of auditions.

As Nicole Forester she landed recurring roles on several television series (*Two and a Half Men*, *Will & Grace*, *Monk*, and *Beverly Hills 90210*), appeared in TV movies of the week, and landed parts in *Simpatico* (with Jeff Bridges and Sharon Stone) and in *Vampires Anonymous*, a film she's probably trying to forget.

Beginning with an episode on November 4, 2005, Nicole played Cassie Layne Winslow on CBS's long-running soap opera, *Guiding Light*, a role she inherited from predecessor Laura Wright. Nicole quickly and permanently made the role of Cassie her own and received Emmy attention for her portrayal.

On April 1, 2009, CBS announced that *Guiding Light* was being canceled because of low ratings. The show taped its final scenes on August 11, 2009.

6. Vacation Assassination

Born in Freeport, Illinois, on September 8, 1841, Charles Julius Guiteau was the fourth of six children of Luther Wilson Guiteau and Jane Howe. He arrived in Ann Arbor to study at the University of Michigan, and lived with his uncle, William Maynard, mayor of the city. But after failing the entrance examinations, he took remedial classes in Latin and algebra at Union High School.

Although he never attended U-M, Guiteau was able to obtain a law license in Chicago, and he started a firm that engaged in little more than bill collecting. An increasingly unstable Guiteau next turned to theology. He published a book called *The Truth* which was almost entirely plagiarized from the work of John Humphrey Noyes, founder of religious sect known as the Oneida Community.

As his interest turned to politics, Guiteau imagined himself largely responsible for James A. Garfield's 1880 election as President and requested an ambassadorship. On July 2, 1881, as President Garfield prepared to leave by train for a vacation with his wife in Long Branch, New Jersey, Guiteau stepped out of the crowd and shot Garfield twice from behind. Without antibiotics at that time, the President endured a painful battle with infections and died eleven weeks after being shot.

Guiteau was found guilty of the murder and hanged on June 30, 1882. Part of his brain remains on display at the Mütter Museum in Philadelphia.

7. Poetic License

In 1921, the great American poet, Robert Frost, accepted a $5,000 fellowship and became the University of Michigan's first Poet-in-Residence. After a brief return to New England in 1923, he returned to U-M for two additional years. (He wrote his most famous work, "Stopping by Woods on a Snowy Evening," between his first and second Ann Arbor tenures.)

Frost had no official teaching obligations and was fond of referring to himself as "Michigan's idle fellow." As he described it, his role was "to do my work and radiate poetic atmosphere for the University."

When it was suggested to Frost that he was as popular a figure on campus as the football coach, Fielding Yost (see **Hurry Up**, page 92), Frost proposed scheduling a poetry reading on a Saturday afternoon during a home football game. "If anyone comes," he explained, "they will be the only one there, because I shall be at the football game."

He later wrote that he had "got to be a good deal more Ann Arboreal than I should suppose I could have at my age. A few people and streets and a lot of the outlying landscape are pretty well incorporated in me."

The Greek Revival house that Robert Frost lived in when he was in Ann Arbor was moved from its foundation and relocated to the Henry Ford Museum in Dearborn.

8. Uferisms

Born in Mt. Lebanon, Pennsylvania, on April 1, 1920, Bob Ufer attended the University of Michigan, played football as a freshman but excelled in track, setting 8 all-time Michigan varsity track records, including the world's quarter mile record, which stood for 5 years and remained a Michigan varsity record for 32 years.

After graduation he started an insurance brokerage in Ann Arbor and became the voice of the University of Michigan football team. From 1945 to 1981, for 363 consecutive games, he was a partisan broadcaster, passionately and unapologetically rooting for the Wolverines. In November of 1976, Ufer was the keynote speaker at Gerald R. Ford's (see **The Appointed One**, page 4) kickoff rally for the Presidency.

He had many familiar so-called "Uferisms," such as referring to Michigan as "Meeechigan," mimicking the pronunciation of coach Fielding Yost (see **Hurry Up**, page 92) and honking loudly on the "Bo-George Patton-Schembechler horn," the actual horn from General Patton's Jeep – three times for a touchdown, two times for a field goal or safety, and once for an extra point.

He often referred to Michigan Stadium (see **The Big House**, page 20) as "The hole that Yost dug, Crisler paid for, Canham carpeted, and Schembechler fills up every Saturday." Bob Ufer lost a long battle with cancer October 26, 1981, nine days after his last broadcast.

9. Big Dig

Born in Ann Arbor on April 1, 1861, William L. Clements was educated in local public schools and entered the University of Michigan in the fall of 1878, graduating with a degree in engineering. He joined his father's firm, the Bay City Industrial Works, manufacturers of steam shovels and cranes, occupying the positions of engineer, superintendent, and manager, and finally president, which position he held for 20 years before his retirement in 1925.

Clements' fortune was made supplying equipment for the construction of the Panama Canal. The first Bay City steam shovel started work on the Culebra cut on November 11, 1904, and by December of 1905 there were more than 100 steam shovels at work, each capable of excavating up to 1200 cubic yards in an eight-hour day.

As his personal wealth grew, Clements cultivated a passion for history and rare books. Beginning in 1920, he made a series of major purchases, concentrating on the discovery, exploration, and colonization of America by Europeans from the 15th through 17th centuries, and late 18th century colonial and revolutionary America. In 1923, he donated his rare book collection to the University of Michigan.

As Clements suffered heavy financial losses during the Great Depression, his health declined, and he died at his home in Bay City in 1934.

10. McNamara's War

Born in San Francisco on June 9, 1916, Robert Strange McNamara earned an MBA from Harvard Business School in 1939, then during World War II, served in the Army Air Forces with the AAF's Office of Statistical Control. In 1946 he joined Ford Motor Company where he worked his way to the top of the Ford hierarchy, and by 1960 became the first company president not directly related to Henry Ford.

During his time with the auto company, McNamara lived in Ann Arbor, commuting 76 miles to Ford Headquarters in Dearborn every day. He and his family resided at 410 Highland Road, a quiet street just off Geddes Road. They were devout members of the First Presbyterian Church and had a strong presence in the university community, regularly attending U-M football and hockey games.

In 1960, McNamara left Ann Arbor for Washington, accepting John F. Kennedy's invitation to serve as Secretary of Defense in the new Administration. Although not especially knowledgeable about defense matters, McNamara applied his skills to the management of the department.

He played a controversial role in the escalation of a conflict that came to be called "McNamara's War." He claimed that if Vietnam came under the influence of communism, then surrounding countries would follow in a "domino effect."

11. Hizzoner

Born in Kalamazoo, Michigan, on March 29, 1917, Samuel James Eldersveld grew up the son of a minister in Muskegon. He graduated from Calvin College in 1938, and received Master's and Ph.D. degrees from the University of Michigan in 1939 and 1946 respectively. A lieutenant in the Navy during World War II, he served as a communications officer in the Philippines, after which he returned to Ann Arbor and joined the U-M faculty, where he taught political science for 54 years.

According to his memoirs, Eldersveld took an interest in local politics because he thought he might one day teach a class on U.S. political parties. In 1957, the "courtly warrior" ran for mayor of Ann Arbor as a Democrat, quite a feat in a city historically dominated by conservative Republicans. Although his wife was opposed to his entry into the contest, Eldersveld convinced her to let him run because he said he had no chance of winning. He became the city's first Democratic mayor since 1929, defeating the Republican incumbent, William Brown, who had been in office since 1945.

Although he continued to teach at the university during his term at City Hall, he was instrumental in the creation of Ann Arbor's Human Relations Commission, committed to eliminating racial discrimination in housing, banking, business, and education.

12. Man in the White Suit

Mark Twain was arguably the most famous person not just in America but in the world when he visited Ann Arbor on December 12, 1872, to lecture the local audience on the topic of humorist Artemus Ward. Besides being responsible for the publication of Twain's first big success, the "Jumping Frog" story, in an eastern magazine in 1865, Ward pioneered the profession of comic lecturing and paved a path for Twain to follow. Ward, whose real name was Charles Farrar Browne, had succumbed to tuberculosis on March 6, 1867, at the age of 32.

Arriving from an appearance the prior evening in Toledo, Ohio, Twain appeared elegantly clad in the trademark white suit that complemented his white mustache, distinctive hair, and of course, an ever-present cigar. He spoke in a slow backwoods drawl, with many strategic pauses, describing Ward's hair as a divided flame and his nose as a cowcatcher. His humorous biography of Ward – more exaggeration than strict historical truth – kept the audience, as reported, "convulsed with laughter for the better part of an hour and a quarter."

For some years, Twain had lost money in various money-making schemes like mining, printing machines, the Charles L. Webster Publishing Co., and *The Mark Twain Self-Pasting Scrap Book*. To recover financially, he embarked on ambitious lecture tours to supplement his writings.

13. Fathers of Invention

Born in Ann Arbor on May 20, 1913, where his father served on the U-M medical school faculty, William Reddington Hewlett attended Stanford University and received a Bachelor of Arts degree in 1934. He also received a master's degree in electrical engineering from the Massachusetts Institute of Technology in 1936. Additionally, he received the degree of Engineer from Stanford University in 1939.

Bill Hewlett met David Packard during their undergraduate days at Stanford. The two engineering classmates became friends and formed a partnership known as the Hewlett-Packard Company in 1939. HP's first product was a resistance-capacitance audio oscillator based on a design developed by Hewlett when he was in graduate school. The company's first "plant" was a small garage in Palo Alto, and the initial capital investment amounted to $538.

During World War II Hewlett headed the electronics section of the New Development Division of the War Department Special Staff. During his final tour of duty, he was on a special U.S. team that inspected Japanese industry immediately after the war.

HP has become one of the world's largest information technology companies, specializing in developing and manufacturing computing, data storage, and networking hardware, designing software and delivering services.

14. Blame The Doors

James Newell Osterberg, Jr. was born on April 21, 1947, in Muskegon, Michigan, the son of Louella (Christensen) and James Newell Osterberg, Sr., a former high school English teacher and baseball coach at Fordson High School in Dearborn. The young boy was raised in a trailer park in Ypsilanti.

Jim Osterberg began his music career as a drummer in an Ann Arbor high school band called the Iguanas (the source of future moniker "Iggy"). Andy Warhol met Iggy at the Ann Arbor Film Festival in 1966 and wrote, "I don't know why he hasn't made it really big; he is so good."

The extreme stage antics of Jim Morrison during a 1967 appearance by The Doors at U-M inspired Iggy to push the boundaries of his own stage persona. His performances would eventually include the stage-dive, rolling around in broken glass, exposing himself to the crowd, and vomiting on stage, among many other exploits.

In 1968, Iggy's band, The Stooges, signed with Elektra Records, following in the footsteps of The Doors, who were Elektra's biggest act at the time (reportedly, Iggy called Moe Howard of the Three Stooges comedy team for permission to call his band "The Stooges.")

Iggy Pop is considered an influential innovator of punk rock and hard rock. In 1980 he published an autobiography called *I Need More*, co-written with Ann Arbor arts patron Anne Weher.

15. He Got Game

Born in Chicago on June 7, 1944, Cazzie Lee Russell played at Carver High School, where his team lost the Illinois state championship by one point. Before Russell arrived in Ann Arbor, U-M had suffered through four losing seasons in a row, but while he was here, he led the Wolverines to three consecutive Big Ten Conference titles (1964-66) and to Final Four appearances in 1964 and 1965.

A 6-foot-5 guard, Russell averaged 24.8 points per game in his sophomore year, 25.7 as a junior, and 30.8 as a senior to lead the University of Michigan to a 65-17 record during his career. He was named an All-American in 1965 and 1966 and was a consensus choice as the 1966 College Player of the Year. His biggest win came in the Final Four as a junior when Michigan defeated Princeton, led by All-American Bill Bradley, as the Wolverines made it to the finals before losing to John Wooden's UCLA team at New York's Madison Square Garden.

When Russell played at Michigan, the basketball games were held at Yost Arena, with seating for less than 2,000 fans. Opened in 1967, 14,000-seat Crisler Arena has been dubbed "The House that Cazzie Built." Russell's number 33 jersey has been retired by the Wolverines.

Russell was the No. 1 overall draft pick in the NBA by the New York Knicks, and he was a key member of New York's 1970 NBA championship team.

16. Snapshot in History

A compact mantle radio called the "Kadette" was introduced to the American market in 1931 by the International Radio Corporation of Ann Arbor. Its plastic case, manufactured for IRC by the Chicago Molded Products Company marked the beginning of a new era in cabinet design as the first set housed in bakelite.

Inspired by the German-made Leica, Charles Albert Verschoor, president of IRC, decided to expand his company with a mass-produced 35mm compact camera. Designed to accommodate Eastman Kodak's new Daylight-Loading Cartridge, the Argus A (named for the hundred-eyed giant in Greek mythology) debuted in 1936 with a list price of ten dollars. More than 30,000 were sold in the first week alone, changing the company's direction. Verschoor sold his radio patents, changed the name of the firm to International Research Corporation, and set about developing a line of cameras.

The Argus C3, introduced in 1939, became the best-selling 35mm camera in the world, and helped popularize the 35mm format. Due to its shape, size, and weight, it is commonly referred to as "The Brick."

After Verschoor's death in 1943, the company became the Vokar Corporation and moved from Ann Arbor to nearby Dexter. The company went bankrupt in 1950.

17. Old Time Rock and Roll

Born in Dearborn, Michigan, on May 6, 1940, Robert Clark Seger lived most of his childhood in Ann Arbor and graduated from Pioneer High School, where he was a member of the track and field team.

Following in the footsteps of his father, a musician (and Ford plant worker) who led a big band in the 40s, Bob wrote his first song and formed his first local band, the Decibels, at age 15. In 1966, he released his first solo single, "East Side Story," which became a regional hit. In 1968, he formed the Bob Seger System and signed with Capitol Records, releasing his debut album, *Ramblin' Gamblin' Man* with the title track climbing to number 17 on the national charts.

He is known as a workhorse Midwestern roots-rocker who dealt with blue-collar themes and toured constantly in support of his frequent album releases. Leader of Bob Seger and the Last Heard, and then later the Bob Seger System, he is best known for his work with the Silver Bullet Band, a group he formed in 1974.

The three albums released between 1976 and 1980, *Night Moves*, *Strangers in Town*, and *Against the Wind*, were the cornerstones of Bob Seger's glory years. His song "Old Time Rock and Roll," is used in a memorable scene from the Tom Cruise film *Risky Business*. Another song, "Like A Rock," was used for many years as theme music for Chevrolet truck commercials.

18. Carmen Sternwood

Born in Ann Arbor on May 28, 1925, Martha MacVicar began her career as a model and cover girl. Her first film role was a small part in *Frankenstein Meets the Wolf Man* in 1941. She played in several films during the early 1940s and was first billed as "Martha Vickers" for her breakthrough film, *The Big Sleep*, starring Humphrey Bogart as detective Philip Marlowe, in which she was cast as Carmen Sternwood, Lauren Bacall's sensuous, thumb-sucking younger sister.

Vickers prances down a curving staircase in short shorts, sashays over to Bogart and says, "You're not very tall, are you?" Bogart replies, "I try to be." She then tries to sit in his lap while he's standing up.

An early cut of *The Big Sleep* is said to show Vickers stealing the spotlight from Bacall. Before the film was released in 1946, the studio had Vickers' sexy scenes cut and more glamorous, sympathetic shots of Bacall inserted, building up the relationship between Bogart and Bacall.

The most famous of Vickers' three husbands was Mickey Rooney, to whom she was wed from 1949 to 1951; husband number two was Paramount producer A. C. Lyles Jr., and number three was polo player Manuel Rojas. Each marriage ended in divorce. She had one son with Mickey Rooney, and two daughters with Rojas. Vickers retired from films after appearing in *Four Fast Guns* in 1960 and died of esophageal cancer at age 46.

19. Bordering on Success

In 1971, University of Michigan undergraduates, Louis and Tom Borders, opened a used bookstore in two rooms above 209 State Street in Ann Arbor, a space previously rented by James "Iggy" Osterberg (see **Blame The Doors**, page 14). In 1981, they bought out the stock of Wahr's, an 80-year-old bookstore that was going out of business at 316 South State, and moved into that location.

Fueled by the Ann Arbor store's success, the Borders brothers opened two more bookstores in Michigan, one in Atlanta, and another in Indianapolis, each using an innovative inventory management software they called BIS (Book Inventory System). Each bookstore had its own customized stock list that automatically adjusted inventory selections based on reader preferences.

In 1988, former Hickory Farms president Robert F. DiRomualdo was hired to run the company, and within three years he opened 14 new stores. In 1992, the brothers sold the company to K-Mart for $200 million, and by 2002, Borders Books was the second most popular bookstore chain in the United States.

The current local store stands at the corner of Liberty and State Streets, in the building once occupied by Jacobson's Department Store. Although not the original location, it is still identified as Borders No. 001.

20. The Big House

The first officially-sanctioned University of Michigan football game was played on May 12, 1883, against the Detroit Industrial Team in a vacant lot in Ann Arbor. The school's first permanent home field site, Regents Field, opened for the 1893 football season with a 6-0 victory over the Detroit Athletic Club. Between 1901 and 1904, the "Point-a-Minute" teams of Fielding Yost (see **Hurry Up**, page 20) went 44-0 at Regents Field, outscoring their opponents 2,821 to 42.

When it became apparent that the Regents Field facilities were no longer adequate to handle the growing crowds at Michigan football games, Detroit businessman and philanthropist Dexter Ferry donated the land immediately north of Regents Field to the university. 18,000-seat Ferry Field was inaugurated with a 28-0 win over Case on October 6, 1906.

In the early 1920s, as athletic director, Yost put a plan in motion that would become Michigan Stadium. Fashioned after the Yale Bowl, 440 tons of reinforcing steel and 31,000 square feet of wire mesh went into building the 44-section, 72-row, 72,000-seat stadium at a cost of $950,000. As the stadium neared completion, Yost requested an additional 10,000 temporary seats for the concourse, and Michigan Stadium opened with a capacity of 84,401 – the largest college owned stadium of any team in the nation.

On Oct. 1, 1927, LaVerne H. "Kip" Taylor was the first man to score at Michigan Stadium as the Wolverines beat Ohio Wesleyan 33-0.

21. Final Resting Place

Beginning in 1844, after years at sea off South America and in the Far East, Dr. Benajah Ticknor called Ann Arbor his home. A self-taught classical scholar, mathematician, philosopher, and diarist, Dr. Ticknor participated in the social and intellectual life of the University community and was sought after for medical opinions. Upon his death in 1859, Ticknor was the first interment in the newly-developed local cemetery, Forest Hill.

A civil engineer named James L. Glenn designed the 65-acre memorial park in the rural or garden style popular in the second half of the 19th century. The belief was that burying and commemorating the dead was best done in a tranquil and beautiful natural setting away from the center of town.

James Morwick built the Gothic stone entrance – the gateway bell was originally rung for funerals. The stone house and office were added in 1874, designed by Gordon W. Lloyd, the preeminent architect of Gothic Revival churches in the Midwest in the 1860s and 1870s.

Many leading citizens of Ann Arbor and distinguished members of the University of Michigan community are laid to rest in Forest Hill. Fielding Yost (see **Hurry Up**, page 92), the grand old man of U-M athletics chose to be buried at Forest Hill, explaining, "I wish to rest where the spirit of Michigan is warmest."

22. Facing Jack Dempsey

New York newspaperman Damon Runyon called him "the old weeping willow from Paw Paw, Michigan." That's where local heavyweight boxer Homer Smith's career began, just west of Kalamazoo, with a bout in the Paw Paw Longwell Opera House. On December 10, 1911, Smith knocked out Art Watkins, a heavyweight from Grand Rapids. It was the beginning of a 17-year professional career, from 1911 to 1928, that would match Smith against a list of fighters that included Sailor Jack Carroll, See Saw Kelly, and Battling Jack Nelson.

Smith's most memorable fight occurred on January 25, 1918, in Racine, Wisconsin, facing off against Jack Dempsey (who was only one year away from becoming world heavyweight champion, a title he would successfully defend from 1919 to 1926). As the match began, the two fighters circled each other. After a brief exchange of punches, Dempsey landed a devastating left to Smith's jaw; he went down hard and was counted out before the end of the first round. In his autobiography, Dempsey referred to Smith as "that clean living kid from Kalamazoo," since Smith never smoke nor drank.

Later in life, Smith worked in an Ann Arbor real estate office, and earned his real estate certification from the University of Michigan at age 71.

23. The Game

The intense rivalry between the University of Michigan and Ohio State didn't begin on the gridiron. It began in 1835 when Michigan claimed a 468-square-mile area that had been surveyed by Ohio at the beginning of its statehood. Militias were mobilized and sent to positions on opposite sides of the Maumee River near Toledo, but besides mutual taunting, there was little interaction between the two forces.

When Michigan sought statehood, it wanted to include the disputed territory within its boundaries, however, Ohio's Congressional delegation was able to halt Michigan's admission to the Union until they gave up their claim.

It was during this dispute that Ohioans branded their adversaries as "wolverines," and while Michiganders liked the evocation of aggressiveness and tenacity, some historians believe the comparison to the insatiable gluttons of the weasel family was an insult by Ohioans. There are no actual wolverines in Michigan.

The inaugural meeting between Ohio State and Michigan at Ann Arbor in 1897 resulted in a 34-0 lopsided Michigan victory over the Buckeyes, the beginning of streak that had U-M winning or tying every match from 1897 to 1912, compiling a 12–0–2 record before the contest was postponed for several years.

The annual game is ranked by ESPN as the greatest North American sports rivalry.

24. "It's the University Girl"

The daughter of a professor at Albion College (where a library was named for her parents), Madelon Louisa Stockwell studied at Kalamazoo College before enrolling at the University of Michigan. In 1870 she entered the sophomore class, and U-M became the first large, prestigious university to admit a woman.

Her admittance was considered by some to be a "dangerous experiment," and she was teased by the other women of Ann Arbor. When she walked by, they would say, "It's the university girl." On the other hand, the men were nice to her, especially fellow student Charles K. Turner, who was seated next to her in class. Upon graduation in 1872, Madelon became Mrs. Charles K. Turner (she taught art and he practiced law). At her death, U-M received a bequest of $10,000 to be used for the education "of three or more women students."

Stockwell Hall, the all-female residence hall named in her honor (and noted for its striking collegiate gothic facades) opened in 1940. After undergoing a $39.6 million renovation, it re-opened in 2009 as a co-ed dormitory.

In 1878, Virginia Watts of Ann Arbor became the first African-American woman to enroll at the University of Michigan; another black woman, Katherine Crawford, received her medical degree from U-M in 1898 and opened a medical practice in Ann Arbor's old 5th ward.

25. Never on Sunday

Born in Muskegon, Michigan, on February 4, 1906, Benjamin Gaylord Oosterbaan began his athletic career at Muskegon High School where he was selected by the *Detroit News* as an All-State end. In his junior year, he led the Muskegon basketball team to a state championship and was named a High School All-American in basketball.

At the University of Michigan, Oosterbaan earned nine letters – three apiece in football, basketball, and baseball. As a senior he was captain, most valuable player, and an All-American in football, Big Ten scoring champion and All-American in basketball, and Big Ten batting average champion in what may be the most dominant three sport performance in any conference in a single year.

After graduation, Oosterbaan declined offers from professional football. As a member of the Dutch Reformed Church, he refused to play on Sundays. Instead, Oosterbaan stayed on at the University of Michigan, first as an assistant coach, then in 1948 as head coach of the football team. Fritz Crisler named Oosterbaan as his successor, describing him as "the best offensive mind in college football." He led the Wolverines to a National Championship in his first season.

Oosterbaan resigned as the head football coach in 1958 and was succeeded by Bump Elliott (see **Bump and Grind**, page 77).

26. Strike Up the Band

He studied violin as a child, graduated from the Beethoven Conservatory of Music in St. Louis, and received degrees from the Chicago Musical College and the Columbia School of Music. William D. Revelli played in silent movie orchestras at theaters in Chicago before accepting a position as supervisor of music at Hobart High School in Hobart, Indiana, in 1925.

Revelli transformed Hobart into one of the best small high school bands in the country, and at a 1931 competition in Tulsa, Oklahoma, the band won its sixth consecutive national championship in a competition that featured John Philip Sousa, the "March King," as one of the judges.

He became director of the University of Michigan bands in 1935. Known on the U-M campus as "The Chief," Revelli was a tough taskmaster. His fierce dedication to excellence and desire for perfection built the university bands into the best in the nation. Revelli once compared himself and his training methods to those of coach Bo Schembechler (see **The Ten-Year War**, page 34).

Revelli's first love was the Symphony Band (larger than the all-male Marching Band), chosen by the Department of State to represent the United States in the first cultural exchange program with the Soviet Union in 1961. After touring Russia and eight other countries for 15 weeks, the trip culminated with a concert at Carnegie Hall.

27. No Stone Unturned

A graduate of the University of Michigan forestry school, Eli Gallup was hired as Ann Arbor Superintendent of Parks in 1919. He would devote the next 45 years to expanding and improving the city's park system, including much of the Huron River corridor where the 69-acre park at Geddes Pond bears his name.

In 1932, Gallup discovered a large Canadian limestone rock deposited by a prehistoric glacier into a gravel pit near Pontiac Trail. Attracted by its size and the glacial scratch marks on its surface, Gallup suggested a public display of the rock in commemoration of George Washington's two-hundredth birthday. With funding from the Daughters of the American Revolution, the rock was lifted with jacks from the Michigan Central Railroad, transported on a heavy-duty Detroit Edison truck, and installed on a triangle of land between Washtenaw and Hill that the city had owned since 1911. Gallup buried a time capsule containing information about 1932 in a lead box on the site, then built a cement pedestal on top of it to hold the rock.

In the mid-1950s, a group of Michigan State hooligans defaced the surface of the stoic monument with the "MSU" insignia. It was quickly painted over in U-M maize and blue, and a tradition was born. Gallup's rock is painted over regularly by students.

28. Trailer-Made

Travel trailers rolled onto the American scene in the 1920s, and campgrounds for "tin can tourists" began popping up around the country. After Harold Kraft was transferred by his employer, Michigan Bell Telephone, from Grand Rapids to Ann Arbor, he started selling trailers part-time. By the mid-1930s, he had a Palace Travel Coach on display at Hob Gainsley's gas station on South University at Forest. For a small kick-back, Gainsley referred prospective buyers to Kraft.

During the Depression, some owners started using their trailers as permanent homes, and in 1939, Michigan became the first state to enact a law regulating trailers used as housing. Stationary trailers were regulated as buildings, while the travel trailer remained under vehicular regulations.

In 1940, Kraft purchased farm land in Pittsfield Township and established the "Ypsi-Ann Trailer Park," the first venture of its kind in the state. He built a cinder-block building for his sales office, including shower stalls, bathrooms, and laundry facilities, since many early trailers didn't include these amenities.

In 1946, he sold the park to Ruby and Sven Keenan, who changed the park's name to "Sunnyside." Kraft continued to sell trailers from a Quonset hut and later co-owned a trailer park in Belleville. In 1958 he retired and moved to Florida. His 1969 obituary described Kraft as a "pioneer in the house trailer industry."

29. Naked Truth

At midnight, on the last day of classes in April of 1986, twelve members of the University of Michigan men's and women's rowing teams and varsity men's track team celebrated by removing their clothes and streaking down South University Avenue.

The "Naked Mile" became a tradition at the university, in which hundreds of students, traditionally graduating seniors, ran across campus naked, while spectators cheered them on, to celebrate the end of the school year. Although technically illegal, it was tolerated by local police until 1998, when authorities began to discourage continuation of the event, fueled in part by concerns over outsiders videotaping the event and selling the recordings online.

In 2000, the teams credited with starting the tradition boycotted the event, declaring they no longer wanted to participate in the Naked Mile. In 2001, the Mile was broadcast live over the Internet by Cyber Management Inc., an Atlanta-based company. Photographers from national media hovered over the event in blimps and helicopters.

The Department of Public Safety estimated that only a dozen students – down from 400 in 2000 and 800 in 1999 – actually participated in the 2001 running. Several students were arrested, while hundreds of other students organized a sit-in to protest the arrests. By 2005, the tradition had all but disappeared.

30. House That Cazzie Built

The home arena for U-M basketball teams, Crisler Arena was constructed in 1967, with seating for 13,751 spectators. It is named for Herbert O. "Fritz" Crisler (see **Wings Over Ann Arbor**, page 39), football coach at Michigan from 1938 to 1947 and athletic director until his retirement in 1968.

The arena is often called "The House that Cazzie Built," a reference to legendary player Cazzie Russell (see **He Got Game**, page 15), who starred on Michigan teams that won three consecutive Big Ten Conference titles from 1964 to 1966. Russell's popularity caused the team's fanbase to outgrow Yost Fieldhouse (now Yost Ice Arena) and prompted the construction of the new facility in 1967.

The arena has also hosted concerts, perhaps most famously, the opening show of Bruce Springsteen's 1981 "The River" Tour, in which Springsteen began the show by completely forgetting the words to "Born to Run," but was rescued by the audience. In the show's encore, local hero Bob Seger (see **Old Time Rock and Roll**, page 17) appeared onstage for a "Thunder Road" duet with Springsteen. Crisler Arena was also the site of the 1971 John Sinclair Freedom Rally (see **Say You Want a Revolution**, page 91).

Crisler Arena was designed by Dan Dworsky (see **Mad Magician**, page 95), a member of the 1948 Rose Bowl team.

31. Towering Achievement

Robert Lurie met Samuel Zell met when both were students at the University of Michigan during the 1960-61 academic year. They became fraternity brothers at Alpha Epsilon Pi, and in 1966, Lurie completed his studies with a Masters of Science in Engineering degree, Zell with a Juris Doctor degree from the Law School.

Lurie and Zell established a realty management service and began buying apartment buildings in Southeastern Michigan. Lurie handled the books, Zell cut the deals, and over 30 years, the two men built a sprawling network of companies that spanned the breadth and depth of American business, including commercial real estate, insurance, vacation cruise lines, agricultural products, drug stores, radio stations, sporting goods, and part-ownership of the Chicago White Sox baseball team and the Chicago Bulls basketball team.

The partnership was cut short when Lurie died of cancer at the age of 48 in 1990. His legacy lives on at the university with the Robert H. Lurie Engineering Center and the 165-foot-tall Lurie Tower, designed by postmodern architect, Charles Willard Moore (U-M '47). Constructed as a poured concrete with a veneer of bricks and ceramic tile and a copper roof, the $5.2 million tower houses a 60-bell carillon. The massive bourdon (largest) bell is the "Robert H. Lurie Bell" and the next six largest bells are inscribed with the names and birth dates of his wife and their six children.

32. Angell's Guardians

A farm boy from Belding, Michigan, Carleton Watson Angell took his first art lessons as a child from a customer on his father's milk route. Angell studied sculpture at the Chicago Art Institute and while in Chicago designed for the American Terra Cotta Company and the Ceramic Company. In 1922 he was hired by the University of Michigan to teach freehand drawing.

In 1926 he was named the Museums Artist for the construction of the Ruthven Museums building, where he contributed many decorative details, including the bronze front doors and the limestone bas-reliefs of animals and naturalists on the facade. The pumas that guard the entryway were installed in 1940.

Angell explained that although lions are often chosen to guard public buildings, he preferred Michigan's native cats. After building scale models to check the proportions, he constructed full-size figures of wood, wire, plaster of Paris, and clay. From these he created plaster molds, which were used to cast the final versions in terrazzo, a stone aggregate.

After sixty years, weathering had caused the pumas to crack and crumble. In order to ensure their preservation, molds were taken of the originals and new pumas were cast in bronze from the molds. The bronze pumas were installed in spring 2007, funded by a donation from alumni Jagdish and Saroj Janveja.

33. House of the Future

At the end of World War II, the American G.I. came home to marry the girl he'd left behind, buy a home, and start a family. But housing construction had virtually stopped during the war years, compounding a critical shortage in residential housing.

In 1947, Chicago industrialist and inventor Carl Strandlund, who had previously designed prefabricated gas stations, obtained a $12.5 million Reconstruction Finance Corporation loan to mass produce pre-fab, porcelain-enameled steel houses with steel framing and steel interior walls and ceiling. His "Lustron House" promised to do for housing what Henry Ford had done for the Model T – make an "Everyman" house. From its plant in Columbus, Ohio, Strandlund's firm sold 2,560 houses between 1948 and 1950, each selling for between $8,500 and $9,500 – about 25 percent less than comparable conventional housing.

Local businessman and Democratic Party leader Neil Staebler secured the rights to the Ann Arbor franchise, but after building nine Lustrons in the city, he decided to switch to more conventional prefabs, finding the opposition to Lustrons "a hornet's nest." With hostility from labor unions, who saw mass production as a threat to workers in the construction industry, government support evaporated, and the Lustron Corporation declared bankruptcy in 1950.

34. The Ten-Year War

Born in Barberton, Ohio, on April 1, 1929, Glenn Edward "Bo" Schembechler, Jr. played college football as a tackle at Miami University in Oxford, Ohio, where in 1949 and 1950 he was coached by Woody Hayes, for whom he served as an assistant coach at Ohio State University in 1952 and from 1958 to 1962.

Schembechler became the University of Michigan's head coach after the 1968 season, succeeding Bump Elliott (see **Bump and Grind**, page 77), and in his first season he led the Wolverines to an upset victory over an Ohio State team coached by his old mentor, Woody Hayes. That win over Ohio State is considered to be one of the greatest upsets in college football history and the most significant win for a Michigan team ever.

Over ten years, Schembechler's teams squared off in a fierce rivalry against Hayes' Buckeye squads. During that stretch, dubbed the "Ten-Year War," the two teams won or shared the Big Ten Conference crown every season and usually each placed in the national rankings.

Between 1976 and 1978, Michigan won the game each year, and Ohio State failed to score a touchdown in each of those contests. Woody Hayes was fired at the end of the 1978 season after punching an opposing player during the Gator Bowl, ending the "War," and giving Schembechler a record of 5-4-1 against Hayes.

35. Spiritual Son

Born in Midland, Michigan, on April 10, 1904, Alden B. Dow attended the Midland Public Schools district, then was sent to the University of Michigan to study engineering in preparation to enter his father's company. But young Alden had a mind of his own, and after three years at U-M, Dow transferred to Columbia University study architecture, graduating in 1931.

After a year and a half of working with the architectural firm of Frantz and Spence in Saginaw, Michigan, Dow was selected to apprentice with Frank Lloyd Wright (see **The Wright Stuff**, page 82) at the Taliesin Estate in Spring Green, Wisconsin, during the summer of 1933.

Wright called Dow his "spiritual son," and following the apprenticeship, Dow opened his own firm, concentrating on residential design using his signature style of Unit Block construction. In this patented method, his designs used white unit blocks, which, though they appeared to be cubes, were actually six-sided rhombuses which gained strength as they were stacked together.

Over the next thirty-six years, Dow designed eighteen Ann Arbor buildings, including 1000 Berkshire Road, built in 1932, the first home in the country with an attached garage facing the street. Dow's design of Ann Arbor City Hall (1961) has been compared to "an inverted wedding cake," "an upside-down carport," and "a poor man's Guggenheim."

36. The Playboy Playwright

Born in Cleveland, Ohio, on May 28, 1882, Avery Hopwood, the son of a butcher, graduated Phi Beta Kappa from the University of Michigan in 1905, and began his career as a journalist for a Cleveland newspaper as its New York correspondent. Within a year, his play, *Clothes*, a collaboration with Channing Pollock, established his reputation as a master of the bedroom farce.

He became the darling of Broadway with plays such as *The Gold Diggers*, *Spanish Love*, *Ladies' Night*, *Streets of New York*, *Fair & Warmer*, *The French Doll*, *Nobody's Widow*, and *The Bat*, his most successful play. In 1920, he had four simultaneous successes running on Broadway.

Hopwood paid his last visit to Ann Arbor in June 1924, and after an evening of reminiscing and heavy drinking at his old fraternity (Phi Gamma Delta), he stumbled outside to an awaiting taxi. He turned before entering the vehicle and shouted, "If you never see me again, remember me this way boys!" When he died four years later, he left one-fifth of his estate to the University of Michigan.

His bequest created the Hopwood Awards, cash prizes awarded to U-M students who perform the best creative work in fields of dramatic writing, fiction, poetry and the essay. The first writing contest was held in 1930-31. Since then, the program has honored almost 3,000 students and dispensed over $1.5 million in prize money.

37. Voiceover

Born in Arkabutla, Mississippi, on January 17, 1931, James Earl Jones grew up in Jackson, Michigan. He remained functionally mute until he reached high school, but with a teacher's encouragement, Jones competed in debates and oratorical contests. As a senior, he won a public-speaking contest and earned a scholarship to the University of Michigan.

It was at U-M where Jones first encountered racial prejudice aimed at him personally. A professor pointed out a misspelling in a paper Jones had written and said: "Why are you trying to be something you're not? You're just a dumb son of a bitch, and you don't belong at this university."

He made his acting debut in a student production of *Deep Are the Roots* by Arnaud d'Usseau and James Gow, in the role of Brett Charles, a black man who grew up in the home of a senator, where his mother was a servant. After graduating in 1953 with a degree in drama, he moved to New York City to pursue an acting career.

After a series of lesser roles, Jones won acclaim in the mid-1960s for his lead role in Shakespeare's *Othello*. In 1964, director Stanley Kubrick cast him in *Dr. Strangelove*, his first movie. In *Star Wars*, his deep basso voice became synonymous with the ultimate in intergalactic evil. Although the role of Darth Vader was played by bodybuilder David Prowse, Jones stepped in for the voiceover — two hours of work for which he was paid $7,000.

38. Past Imperfect

Born in Chicago on June 11, 1905, Richard Albert Loeb was the son of a wealthy Jewish lawyer who went on to become a senior executive with Sears and Roebuck. Loeb was extremely intelligent and was admitted to the University of Chicago at age fourteen as a result of skipping numerous grades. It was there that he became "firm friends" with Nathan Leopold, another brilliant, rich young man. In 1921, Loeb transferred to the University of Michigan, and in June of 1923, he became the youngest graduate in the university's history.

Leopold and Loeb reunited in Chicago, where they became obsessed with the idea of "the perfect crime," cold bloodedly planning a murder for the thrill of getting away with it. On May 21, 1924, the two men rented a car, obscured its number plates and set out in search of a victim. Fourteen-year-old Bobby Franks was lured into the car, hit over the head with a chisel by Loeb. After hiding the body, they delivered a ransom note to the boy's father.

During police questioning, their alibis fell apart, and despite an effort by Clarence Darrow, the country's foremost criminal defense lawyer, Leopold and Loeb each received a life sentence for the murder and an additional 99 years each for the kidnapping. While serving his sentence in Joliet Penitentiary on September 11, 1924, Loeb was killed by his cellmate.

39. Wings Over Ann Arbor

Born in Earlville, Illinois, on January 12, 1899, Herbert Orin Crisler hit the books instead of participating in sports during high school, entering the University of Chicago on an academic scholarship. At Chicago, he played football under Amos Alonzo Stagg, who nicknamed him "Fritz" after Fritz Kreisler, a renown violinist of the era. He became an all-around athletic star, winning a total of nine varsity letters, three each in football, baseball and basketball teams.

In 1930, Crisler was hired as the head football coach at the University of Minnesota, then as head football coach at Princeton from 1932 to 1937 where he compiled a record of 35-9-5. When he took over as head coach at Michigan in 1938, Crisler introduced the distinctive winged football helmet, which has since become one of the symbols of Michigan Wolverines athletics programs.

The Michigan helmet, similar to the headwear Crisler first used at Princeton, made a successful debut in the 1938 season opener against Michigan State. The Wolverines defeated the Spartans 14-0 behind two touchdown runs by sophomore Paul Kromer to gain their first win over Michigan State in four years.

The winged design simply took advantage of features of a helmet the Spalding sporting goods company had advertised in the 1937 edition of the *Official Intercollegiate Football Guide*. Crisler's 1938 innovation at Michigan was to paint the helmet maize and blue.

40. Yeoman Janice Rand

Born in Ann Arbor on April 1, 1930, Mary Ann Chase was adopted by the Whitney family who named her Grace Elaine Whitney. She began an entertainment career as a singer on Detroit's WJR ("from the Golden Tower of the Fisher Building") at the age of fourteen, calling herself Lee Whitney. Eventually she became known as Grace Lee Whitney.

By her late teens, she was working in Chicago nightclubs, opening for Billie Holiday and Buddy Rich, and later touring with the Spike Jones and Fred Waring Bands.

After appearing on Broadway in *Top Banana* with Phil Silvers and Kaye Ballard, Whitney was cast as a member of the all-female band in Billy Wilder's classic comedy *Some Like It Hot*, released in 1959. She shared several scenes with Jack Lemmon, Tony Curtis, and Marilyn Monroe, including the famous "upper berth" sequence.

In 1966, Whitney would boldly go "where no man has gone before." *Star Trek* creator Gene Roddenberry cast her in the role of Yeoman Janice Rand, the personal assistant to Captain James T. Kirk. She reprised her role as Janice Rand in *Star Trek: The Motion Picture*, *Star Trek III: The Search for Spock*, *Star Trek IV: The Voyage Home*, and *Star Trek VI: The Undiscovered Country*. To celebrate the 30th anniversary of the franchise, she returned in the 1996 *Star Trek: Voyager* episode "Flashback" along with George Takei.

41. The Big Chill

Born in Miami, Florida, on January 14, 1949, and raised in Morgantown, West Virginia, Lawrence Kasdan graduated from the University of Michigan with an M.A. in Education, originally planning on a career as an English teacher. Unable to find a teaching position, he became an advertising copywriter, a profession he labored at for five years, first in Detroit and then in Los Angeles, where he tried his hand at screenplays.

Kasdan's introduction into the film business came in the mid-1970s when he sold his script for *The Bodyguard* to Warner Brothers. In 1979, George Lucas commissioned Kasdan to complete the screenplay for *The Empire Strikes Back*, then for *Raiders of the Lost Ark* and the last installment of the *Star Wars* trilogy, *Return of the Jedi*. Kasdan made his directing debut in 1981 with *Body Heat*, which he also wrote.

His 1983 film, *The Big Chill*, tells the story of seven University of Michigan graduates who reconnect via their shared college friend's funeral and which often references U-M during the sixties. Kasdan said the film's title "refers to the experience of going out into the world after the warm embrace of living in Ann Arbor for four years."

The Big Chill went on to earn Oscar nominations for Glenn Close (Best Actress), for Best Original Screenplay, and for Best Picture.

42. Spin the Cube

Born in Highland Park, Illinois, on August 9, 1914, Bernard J. "Tony" Rosenthal took sculpture classes at the Art Institute of Chicago during high school and decided on his career after seeing plaster reproductions of the work of Ukrainian avant-garde sculptor Alexander Archipenko. He earned a B.F.A. from the University of Michigan in 1936.

Rosenthal is probably best known for his 8-foot-square cube, mounted on a corner, on display at Astor Place in downtown Manhattan. Titled "Alamo," it was the first permanent contemporary outdoor sculpture installed in New York City (1967). The cube is made of Cor-Ten steel and weighs about 1,800 pounds.

Ann Arbor is the home of Alamo's sister, "Endover," located at Regents Plaza, donated by the U-M class of 1965 and installed in 1968. Although seemingly massive and immovable, the cube actually rotates on its vertical axis, given a gentle push. Campus legend says that the president of the university gives it a ceremonial push each morning on the way to his office in order to get the school day under way.

The local cube rotates on a pivot sunken into the ground, as opposed to the pivot of the Alamo, which is on a separate platform. Rosenthal preferred the Ann Arbor cube to the New York version because he was able to revise and improve the original design.

43. Alumni Chapter of the Moon

Apollo 15 flew to the moon from July 26 to August 7, 1971, with astronauts Col. David R. Scott (commander), Maj. Alfred Worden (command module pilot), and Col. James Irwin (lunar module pilot) aboard. It was the ninth manned mission in the Apollo program, the fourth mission to land on the Moon and the eighth successful manned mission.

It was the first of what were termed "J missions," long duration stays on the moon with more of a focus on science than had been possible on previous missions. It was the first mission where the lunar rover was used (Scott and Irwin spent 18 hours and 37 minutes exploring the moon's surface in their electronic moonbuggy). And it was the first flight in which the entire crew was from the same university.

All three astronauts on the all-Air Force crew received either an honorary degree or Master's degree from the University of Michigan, including Scott's honorary degree, awarded in the Spring of 1971, just months before the launch. Scott, in fact, did attend the University of Michigan, but left before graduating to accept an appointment to West Point. The astronauts carried three U-M items: a miniature of the school flag, a miniature of the Department of Aerospace Engineering seal, and a charter of the "U-M Alumni Chapter of the Moon," which was left on the moon's surface.

44. America's Corner Store

As a young man, Charles Rudolph Walgreen became a druggist's apprentice in his hometown of Dixon, Illinois. In 1893, he moved to Chicago where he worked at Isaac Blood's pharmacy. Then, in 1901, when Blood retired, Walgreen bought the store from him, and in 1909, he opened a second location.

His son, born in Chicago on March 4, 1906, Charles Rudolph Walgreen, Jr. grew up in the family business. "Chuck" worked as a delivery boy at his father's second store. At the age of 11, he was making banana splits behind the marble-top soda fountain in one of his father's nine drug stores.

He considering a career in architecture, but with his father's encouragement, Chuck entered the University of Michigan School of Pharmacy. By the time he graduated in 1928, there were 397 Walgreens in 87 cities, and he took turns on the store opening crew, in the ice cream plant, and in personnel, sales, manufacturing, purchasing and real estate before becoming vice president in 1933, executive assistant to his father in 1935 and president shortly before the senior Walgreen's death in 1939.

In the 1950s, he redefined the retail drug business, converting the stores from clerk-assisted shopping to self-service. During his tenure, annual sales grew from $72 million to $817 million.

Shortly before his death, Charles Rudolph Walgreen, Jr. donated ten million dollars to U-M, a gift that supported the building of Walgreen Drama Center.

45. Hail to the Victors

As a sophomore at the University of Michigan, Louis Elbel tied the world record for the 40 yard dash. But that's not what places Elbel in the hearts of generations of Wolverines.

By the fall of 1898, the presence of the band at football games had become an indispensable part of Michigan tradition. After Michigan's season-ending come-from-behind victory against the University of Chicago, a post game celebration began in the streets of Chicago. Leading the festivity was the University of Michigan Band, and among the revelers was Elbel who was not convinced that a popular ragtime favorite, "There'll Be a Hot Time in the Old Town Tonight," was an appropriate school song. His own composition, "The Victors," first performed in public in 1899, became Michigan's official fight song. Elbel's tune was declared by John Philip Sousa, conductor of the Marine Band, as "the greatest college fight song ever written."

As President, U-M alumnus Gerald R. Ford (see **The Appointed One**, page 4) often had the Naval band play the fight song prior to state events instead of "Hail to the Chief." He selected the song to be played during his December 2006 funeral procession at the U.S. Capitol. The Michigan Marching Band performed a slow-tempo variation of the fight song one final time, for his last ride from the Gerald R. Ford International Airport in Grand Rapids.

46. Commie High

Established in 1972, Community High School is a public alternative school serving grades 9 through 12. It was one of the first public magnet schools in the country, offering students a smaller alternative to Ann Arbor's three large comprehensive high schools. Considered a unique jewel of the school district, it remains one of the nation's few survivors among the wave of experimental high schools that were founded in the 1970s.

Founded on a progressive "school-without-walls" concept, CHS is not restricted to a particular student population (such as "gifted" or "underachieving" students), and its loose attendance policy is more similar to those of colleges than those at most high schools. The school encourages students to interact with the surrounding community, primarily through its open campus and Community Resources Program, an avenue for students to design their own courses for credit through experiential learning projects in the Ann Arbor area. Students participate in school governance and staff hiring.

With its reputation as a quirky, counter-culture school, CHS is nicknamed "Commie High," abandoning many typical features of traditional high schools, including interscholastic sports programs, valedictorians, dress codes, detention, hall passes, or bells to announce the change of classes.

47. The Mahatma

Born in Stockdale, Ohio, on December 20, 1881, the second of three sons to Jacob Franklin and Emily Rickey, Branch Wesley Rickey was a catcher on the baseball team at Ohio Wesleyan University and, in 1903, signed a contract with Terre Haute, Indiana, of the Class B Central League, making his professional debut on June 20. He sustained an injury to his throwing arm and was forced to retire as a player after just one year, spending the following two seasons coaching baseball and football at Allegheny College.

In 1910, Rickey entered law school at the University of Michigan, and by the following spring he was hired as U-M's baseball coach, the administration convinced he could handle both his course load and coach a varsity team. After home games, Rickey often piled the team into his Chalmers convertible for excursions around Ann Arbor. He also found time to assist Coach Yost (see **Hurry Up**, page 92) on the football field.

Rickey's many achievements and deep Christian faith earned him the nickname "Mahatma." In 1917, as president of the St. Louis Cardinals, he created the modern minor league system. In 1943 he became president and general manager of the Brooklyn Dodgers where he broke a long-standing race barrier by hiring Jackie Robinson, the first black player in major league baseball.

48. Ambush Journalism

Born in Brookline, Massachusetts, on May 9, 1918, Myron Leon Wallace was the son of an immigrant father who ran a wholesale grocery business and later became an insurance broker. The young man showed some interest in sports and music, but found his true calling when he first walked into the campus radio station at the University of Michigan. He appeared as a guest on the popular radio quiz show *Information Please* on February 7, 1939, during his senior year. Upon graduation from U-M, Wallace hit the airwaves as a "rip-and-read" reporter at WOOD in Grand Rapids for $20 a week. By the 1940s he was working as a news writer and announcer for the radio station of the *Chicago Sun*.

During World War II, Wallace served as a communications officer in the U.S. Navy. He returned to Chicago after the war, and became a news reporter for radio station WMAQ. By now he had adopted the nickname "Mike," and as Mike Wallace he was to become one of America's best-known broadcasters. Beginning on September 24, 1968, audiences tuned in to see Wallace and company expose fraud and corruption on CBS's *60 Minutes*. Wallace's confrontational, provocative style was dismissed by some as "ambush journalism," and a few of the program's targets filed lawsuits against CBS, but not one was ever prosecuted successfully.

Wallace has contributed $1 million to a U-M program to establish fellowships a year for international journalists.

49. Doctor on TV

Born in Novi, Michigan, on October 23, 1969, Sanjay Gupta is the son of Subhash and Damyanti Gupta who moved from India to Michigan to work as engineers for the Ford Motor Company in Dearborn in the 1960s. His mother was the first female engineer to work at Ford.

Gupta attended Novi High School, received his B.S. degree in biomedical sciences at the University of Michigan, his M.D. from the University of Michigan Medical Center. He was part of Inteflex, a 6-year program combining pre-medical and medical school that accepted students directly from high school. He completed his residency in neurological surgery within the University of Michigan Health System in 2000.

As CNN's chief medical correspondent he has become a media personality on health-related issues, hosting the network's weekend health program *Sanjay Gupta, M.D.*, and making frequent appearances on their *American Morning*, *Larry King Live*, and *Anderson Cooper 360*.

In addition to his work for CNN, Gupta is a member of the staff and faculty at the Emory University School of Medicine. He is associate chief of neurosurgery at Grady Memorial Hospital, the public hospital for the city of Atlanta, where he regularly performs surgeries. He is a member of the American Association of Neurological Surgeons, Congress of Neurological Surgeons, and the Council on Foreign Relations.

50. Man's Man

Born in Grand Rapids, Michigan, on December 5, 1903, Arnold Gingrich graduated from the University of Michigan in 1925 with a Phi Beta Kappa Key and became an advertising copy writer. In 1931, while he was creating copy for Kuppenheimer Clothes and writing radio scripts in his spare time, he was asked to become the editor of *Apparel Arts* (now *Gentleman's Quarterly*) in Chicago.

In 1933, Gingrich and partner David A. Smart created their own quarterly merchandise catalog, free to customers of clothing manufacturers. They considered calling the magazine *Trend*, *Stag*, *Beau*, *Trim*, or *Town and Campus*, but settled on *Esquire*, inspired by the "Esq." on the stationery of the lawyer hired to check whether those other titles were taken. *Esquire* was a success from its first issue and went monthly the following year.

Its breakthrough editorial mix of men's fashion, scantily clad women, and well-known authors (F. Scott Fitzgerald, Ernest Hemingway, William Faulkner, John Steinbeck, Thomas Wolfe, Truman Capote, Norman Mailer) would eventually inspire an ambitious young writer in *Esquire's* promotion department named Hugh M. Hefner to fantasize about starting his own magazine. When *Esquire* moved its headquarters from Chicago to New York City in the early 1950s, Hef stayed behind and launched *Playboy*.

51. The Flying Shithouse

When events began happening in Europe that would eventually lead to World War II, the American government began to speed-up aircraft production, and in April of 1941, ground was broken for construction of an airplane factory on the outskirts of Ann Arbor.

Fields of a sleepy hamlet called Willow Run were cleared for construction of the plant, designed by architect Albert Kahn (see **World's Largest Megaphone**, page 62). The Pentagon tapped Henry Ford's production chief, Charles Sorenson, to design an auto-style assembly line to manufacture the B-24 bomber, workhorse of the U.S. Army Air Force, unaffectionately known to its crews as "the flying shithouse."

Nine hundred men and women worked night and day seven days a week to design the critical tooling. More than 30,000 metal stamping dies were ultimately required for the bomber's 1,225,000 parts. Eventually 14,000 workers were housed in temporary dormitory-style housing, tents, garages, and trailers. Many larger single-family homes in Ann Arbor were divided into rental rooms or apartments. By August 1944, Willow Run was turning out a B-24 every hour (it later got the time down to 55 minutes), and all told, it produced 9,000 of them.

After the war ended, Ford chose not to buy Willow Run from the government. The plant was sold to Kaiser-Fraser for production of automobiles, then later to General Motors making automatic transmissions.

52. Heart of the Matter

Bruce D. Roth received his bachelor's degree from St. Joseph's College, Philadelphia, in 1976. After receiving his Ph.D. in organic chemistry from Iowa State University in 1981, he spent a year as a Postdoctoral Fellow at the University of Rochester, then joined Parke-Davis of Warner-Lambert Company as a medicinal chemist in 1982. In 1984, he was promoted to senior scientist at the company's research facility in Ann Arbor, working on a class of compounds, originally extracted from fungi, that held the promise of lowering cholesterol, averting heart disease and premature death.

It was in his Ann Arbor lab where Roth first synthesized atorvastatin, the molecule that became Lipitor, the most commonly prescribed drug to lower cholesterol. For his discovery, Roth received the 1997 Warner-Lambert Chairman's Distinguished Scientific Achievement Award, the 1999 Inventor of the Year Award from the New York Intellectual Property Law Association, and the 2003 American Chemical Society Award for Creative Invention.

In addition to his discovery of atorvastatin, Roth is the inventor or co-inventor of 42 patents and the author or co-author of 48 manuscripts and 35 published abstracts. He also served as an adjunct professor in the Department of Medicinal Chemistry at the University of Michigan.

53. Rebels with a Cause

His parents named him after former Wisconsin governor, congressman and senator Robert "Fighting Bob" LaFollette, Progressive Party candidate for President in 1924. Robert Alan Haber grew up in Ann Arbor and entered the University of Michigan in 1954, planning a career as a chemist. In 1960, he was elected president of a small group of student activists called SDS (Students for a Democratic Society). Its socialist-progressive manifesto was adopted at the organization's first convention in 1962, based on an earlier draft by staff member Tom Hayden, editor of the U-M student newspaper (and later the husband of Jane Fonda).

After teaching for several years in a progressive alternative school in Ann Arbor, Bill Ayers turned his energy full time to stopping the war in Vietnam and became a regional organizer for SDS, then internal education secretary. In 1965, Ayers joined a picket line protesting a local pizzeria for refusing to seat African Americans.

While in graduate school at U-M, Todd Gitlin became coordinator of SDS's Peace Research and Action Project. He helped organize the first national demonstration against the Vietnam War, held in Washington, D. C., on April 17, 1965, with 25,000 participants, as well as the first civil disobedience directed against American corporate support for the apartheid regime in South Africa.

SDS expanded rapidly in the mid-1960s before dissolving at its last convention in 1969.

54. Object of Desire

The story of the Little Brown Jug begins early in the last century with the fabled "point-a-minute" Michigan football squads, coached by Fielding Yost (see **Hurry Up**, page 92). His boys had won 28 straight games heading into Minneapolis in 1903 to face the University of Minnesota team.

Before the game, student manager Thomas B. Roberts was sent out to purchase a new container for water, since Yost suspected that Gopher fans might attempt to contaminate his team's water supply. Roberts returned with a five-gallon earthenware jug from a local variety store.

When the underdog Golphers tied the score at 6-6, fans stormed stormed the field in celebration, causing the game to be called with two minutes remaining on the clock. The Wolverines walked off the field, leaving the jug behind. Inspired by the popular song of the era, "Little Brown Jug," L. J. Cooke, head of the Minnesota athletics department, had the jug painted brown and commemorated the game by lettering "Michigan Jug – Captured on October 31, 1903" along with the score "Michigan 6, Minnesota 6." When Yost sent a letter asking Minnesota to return the jug, Cooke wrote back, "if you want it, you'll have to win it."

Painting the victories of each team on the Little Brown Jug represents the oldest rivalry trophy in American college football. Michigan holds the advantage in the series, 66-22-3.

55. Give Earth a Chance

The "Environmental Teach-In," organized by a group of U-M natural science students from March 11 to 14, 1970, provided a model for the first national Earth Day held the following month, on April 22. Calling their group ENACT (Environmental Action for Survival), members ranged from quiet lab types to veterans of SDS (see **Rebels with a Cause**, page 53).

Across the country, eyes turned toward Ann Arbor, watching with great interest. More than sixty major media outlets covered the teach-in, including all three American television networks and a film crew from Japan

Organizers booked Crisler Arena for speeches by Senator Gaylord Nelson, Michigan governor William Milliken, radio personality Arthur Godfrey, and ecologist Barry Commoner. Music was supplied by Gordon Lightfoot and the Chicago cast of *Hair*. They held field trips, clean-ups, and debates. Protests and demonstrations included the mock trial of a '59 Ford that was smashed to pieces by a crowd of sledgehammer-wielding students.

Over four days, an estimated 50,000 people took part in ENACT's event, an astonishing success that fueled enthusiasm for national Earth Day, which drew some 20 million participants four weeks later and transformed environmentalism into a movement of historic importance.

56. Strange Case of H. H. Holmes

Born in Gilmantown, New Hampshire on May 16, 1860, Herman Webster Mudgett, son of Levi Horton Mudgett, the local postmaster, married his childhood sweetheart at the age of twenty, then moved to Ann Arbor to attend medical school at the University of Michigan.

He boosted his student allowance by body snatching — stealing corpses from the medical school laboratory, rendering them unrecognizable with acid, then collecting on the life insurance policies he had previously taken out under fictitious names. He got away with several of these frauds before a night watchman caught him removing a female corpse. He was expelled from the university for "unusual activities."

In 1886, he left Ann Arbor, abandoned his wife and infant son, and turned up in Chicago under the alias, Dr. Henry Howard Holmes. By 1893 he opened a rooming house for visitors to the Chicago World's Fair. He was arrested when police discovered he was systematically killing and robbing his guests.

On the afternoon of November 16, 1894, Holmes was arrested in Boston as he was preparing to leave the country by steamship. He was put on trial for murder, and confessed to 27 murders and six attempted murders. On May 7, 1896, America's first serial killer was hanged, then buried in a coffin filled with cement, in order to discourage souvenir hunters.

57. High Hopes

The Michigan Daily, the student newspaper at the University of Michigan, gained national press coverage by urging the legalization of marijuana as early as 1967. Since then, the city of Ann Arbor has enacted some of the most lenient laws on marijuana possession in the United States. These include measures approved in a 1972 city council ordinance, a 1974 voter referendum making possession of small amounts of the substance merely a civil infraction subject to a small fine, and a 2004 referendum on the use of medical marijuana.

The country's most liberal marijuana enforcement provisions were a reaction to the highly punitive state penalties, which provided for a year's imprisonment for possession of two ounces or less, four years' imprisonment for the sale of marijuana, and harsher penalties for repeat offenses. These unusually strict penalties received national attention when poet and activist John Sinclair was sentenced to ten years in prison for possession of two joints, a sentence that sparked the historic Crisler Arena rally in December 1971 (see **Say You Want a Revolution**, page 91).

Since then, the "Hash Bash" has become an annual event (on the first Saturday in April) to commemorate the occasion and support the reform of marijuana laws.

58. Alma Mater

On March 3, 1805, President Thomas Jefferson appointed Augustus Brevoort Woodward as the Michigan Territory's first Chief Justice. In that position, he soon focused himself on science (a life-long interest) and the establishment of a university based on the model of the University of Virginia, founded by his friend Jefferson. It has been said that Woodward was among the first to recognize the coming of the scientific age.

With Reverend John Montieth and Father Gabriel Richard, Woodward drafted a charter for an institution he called the "Catholepistemiad" or the "University of Michigania." On August 26, 1817, the Governor and Judges of the Michigan Territory signed the university act into law. Although originally planned for Lansing, what would become the University of Michigan was established in Ann Arbor in 1837 thanks to "Boy Governor" Stevens T. Mason (elected at age 24, the youngest-ever state governor in American history).

The first classes were held in 1841, with six freshmen and a sophomore, taught by two professors. Eleven students graduated in the first commencement in 1845. By 1866, enrollment increased to 1,205 students, many of whom were Civil War veterans, and women were first admitted in 1870 (see **"It's the University Girl"** page 24). In 1866, U-M became the largest university in the country, with 1205 enrolled students.

59. Egghead and the Hourglass

Born in New York City on October 17, 1915, Arthur Asher Miller was the son of Isidore Miller, a clothing manufacturer who went broke in the great economic Depression of the 1930s. The family was forced to move from a costly apartment in Manhattan to a small house in Brooklyn.

After graduating from high school in 1932, Miller worked in an auto parts warehouse to earn enough money to attend the University of Michigan. Arriving in Ann Arbor by bus, Miller went to work as a dishwasher and as reporter and night editor on *The Michigan Daily* to help pay his expenses while he studied journalism. In 1936, he changed his major to English after winning the Hopwood Award in Drama for his play, *No Villain*.

After graduation, U-M Professor Kenneth Thorpe Rowe, who taught Shakespeare and modern drama, connected Miller with people in the show-business industry. *Death of a Salesman*, produced on Broadway in 1949, ran for 745 performances, winning both the Tony Award and the Pulitzer Prize for drama. On July 1, 1956, Miller wed Hollywood bombshell Marilyn Monroe, a marriage that lasted four and half years.

In October, 2000, in celebration of his 85th birthday, the university held an international symposium on his work and broke ground for a theater that was named after him.

60. Sweet Victory

By the early 1890s, although the University of Michigan football team had piled up impressive victories, they had yet to prove themselves against any of the elite Eastern football teams. In 1894, led by head coach William McCauley, the Wolverines scheduled a home-and-away series with Cornell, a team led by captain Glenn Scobey "Pop" Warner.

The first of the two contests against Cornell was played in Ithaca, New York, on November 3rd. While the Michigan team, referred to in the press as "gridiron giants," outweighed the Cornell boys by an average of five pounds, the Cornellians were reported to have "greater skill and agility." Betting in advance of the game was 5 to 1 that Cornell would win and 2 to 1 that Michigan would not score. Cornell prevailed, 22 to 0.

The teams met for a rematch on November 24th, this time at the Detroit Athletic Club Field in Detroit. The Michigan players paraded down Woodward Avenue upon arrival, with the Michigan colors "everywhere visible." Two-thousand students traveled from Ann Arbor to watch the game on a cold, overcast afternoon. Michigan held Cornell scoreless in the second half and won the game, 12 to 4. The win over Cornell marked the first time in collegiate football history that a western school defeated an established power from the east.

Michigan closed the 1894 season with a victory over Amos Alonzo Stagg's University of Chicago Maroons.

61. Company Changes Its Tune

In 1867, nineteen-year-old Ira Grinnell began selling sewing machines in Ann Arbor. Within five years, his offerings expanded to include Etsey organs and other musical instruments. Grinnell opened a second store in Ypsilanti, then moved the business to Detroit where he was joined by younger brothers Clayton and Herbert.

In 1901, the firm began manufacturing pianos, a move that met with immediate success. In 1908 the Grinnells built a manufacturing plant in Holly, Michigan, touted as "the largest piano factory on the earth." Pianos were sold exclusively in company-owned stores, offering 15 models of upright and player pianos in a choice of mahogany, walnut, oak, ebony and fruitwood.

The Grinnell brothers became fascinated with the automobile industry emerging in and around Detroit, and in 1910 they introduced an electric-powered car, a five-seater closed coupe the company claimed to have a 90-mile range per charge. The vehicle sold for $2,800.

After managing the Grinnell music store in Lansing for eight years, Sydney J. Guest was summoned to Detroit in the fall of 1912 to manage the faltering Grinnell Electric Car Company. A year later, auto manufacture was discontinued, and the brothers decided to focus on the musical instrument business. The company introduced a line of spinet, console and apartment-size baby grand pianos during the 1930s and 1940s, and the firm continued to flourish until the early 1960s.

62. World's Largest Megaphone

One of the University of Michigan's most venerable buildings, Hill Auditorium was hailed as a "monument to perfect acoustics" when it opened in 1913. It was named in honor of Arthur Hill, regent of the university from 1901 to 1909, who bequeathed $200,000 for construction an auditorium "suitable for superior musical performances and large enough for a gathering of the entire student body."

Albert Kahn of Detroit, who also designed many of the classic buildings at U-M, including the Burton Tower, Hatcher Graduate Library, and Clements Library, determined that every seat should be situated so that even a whisper from the stage could be heard.

Kahn enlisted acoustical engineer Hugh Tallant, who suggested building the auditorium in the shape of a megaphone to allow a lecturer on stage to address an audience of up to 4,000 without a microphone. (The applause of the audience was equally magnified back to the stage, making Hill a favorite venue for performers).

Curved surfaces served to prevent diffusion, and unwanted reflections were avoided by padding the rear walls and the rear part of the side walls. To prevent outside noise from penetrating the auditorium, a combination of solid brick exterior wall, four-inch air space, and four-inch hollow brick interior wall was used.

63. Doctor Death

Born in Pontiac, Michigan, on May 26, 1928, Jack Kevorkian, the son of Armenian immigrants, graduated from Pontiac Central High School with honors in 1945. In 1952, he graduated from the University of Michigan Medical School in Ann Arbor.

Kevorkian started advertising in Detroit newspapers in 1987 as a physician consultant for "death counseling." In 1991 the State of Michigan revoked his medical license and made it clear that given his actions, he was no longer permitted to practice medicine or to work with patients. Between 1990 and 1998, Kevorkian assisted in the deaths of 130 terminally ill people.

Merian Frederick, an Ann Arbor activist and patron of the arts, contracted Lou Gehrig's disease in 1989. On October 22, 1993, no longer able to speak and able to write only a few lines at a time, she visited Kevorkian's apartment in Royal Oak. Kevorkian was acquitted of killing her at a 1996 trial, and in that same year a group called "Merian's Friends" was formed to solicit signatures for a ballot initiative to "provide a better alternative" for others facing lingering death.

Attorney Geoffrey Fieger (B.A. and M.A. from U-M) defended Kevorkian in his six murder trials. Kevorkian choose to represent himself in his last trial and went to prison for nine years.

64. Kidnapped!

Born in Ann Arbor on October 6, 1977, Jill Carroll attended Huron High School where she was a star swimmer, winning a swimming scholarship to the University of Massachusetts.

Carroll's interest in journalism began in college. After graduating from U-Mass in 1999, she briefly worked for States New Service in Washington, then earned an internship with *The Wall Street Journal*. In 2002, she left the *Journal* to follow her interest in the Middle East. As a reporter for the English-language *Jordan Times* in 2002, she began to study Arabic.

After the American-led invasion in March 2003, Carroll headed to Iraq as a freelancer, and by 2005, she was on regular assignment for *The Christian Science Monitor* in Baghdad. On January 7, 2006, she was abducted at gunpoint by Sunni Muslim insurgents, and her translator, Allan Enwiya, was murdered. On January 30, Al-Jazeera satellite network aired a videotape of Carroll wearing an Islamic head scarf and pleading for the release of women Iraqi prisoners.

On March 30, after 82 days in captivity, she was dropped off in a western neighborhood of Baghdad at midday. "I don't know what happened," she said. "They just came to me and said, 'Okay, we're letting you go now.'"

In 2008, Carroll became a firefighter with the Fairfax County (Virginia) Fire and Rescue Department.

65. "Haven of Quiet"

Ossian Cole Simonds was born near Grand Rapids, Michigan, in 1855. Although he was educated as a civil engineer at the University of Michigan, he preferred to call himself a landscape gardener. It was his strong conviction that the best landscape design is inspired by nature, informed by local landforms, and constructed using indigenous plant materials.

In 1907, Walter Hammond Nichols and his wife, Esther Blanche Connor Nichols donated their Ann Arbor property to a partnership between the university and the city for the development of a public park to be designed by Simonds. (After earning a degree in chemistry from U-M, Walter Nichols operated a local fruit farm. He left Ann Arbor for Boulder, Colorado, where he became vice-president of the Mercantile Bank & Trust Company).

With the addition of adjoining land from George P. Burns and Detroit Edison, the 123-acre site became the Nichols Arboretum, with overlooks and trails through woods and fields, including a stroll along the Huron River.

During the 1920s, automobiles, sledders, and skiers began to inflict serious damage on the arboretum. By the mid-1930s, cars were banned and WPA workers laid out over three miles of new hiking trails. The trees grew, wildflowers multiplied, and the arboretum came to fulfill its promise as a "haven of quiet."

66. People's Republic of Ann Arbor

Humorist Garrison Keillor once described Ann Arbor as "a city where people discuss socialism, but only in the fanciest restaurants."

During the 1960s and 1970s, the city earned a reputation not only as a center for liberal politics, but a venue for left-wing activism. Ann Arbor served as a hub for the civil-rights movement, the anti-Vietnam War movement, and a student movement led by the leading radicals of the era (see **Rebels with a Cause**, page 53).

The first major meetings of the national left-wing campus group, Students for a Democratic Society, took place in Ann Arbor in 1960. In 1965, the city was home to the first U.S. teach-in against the Vietnam War. During the ensuing fifteen years, many countercultural and New Left enterprises sprang up and developed large constituencies within the city. These influences washed into municipal politics during the early and mid-1970s when student-supported representatives on the city council seats fought for decriminalizing marijuana possession (see **High Hopes**, page 57).

Former U-M student Alden B. Dow's (see **Spiritual Son**, page 35) design of the Fleming Administration Building, completed in 1968, included narrow windows, all located above the first floor, and a fortress-like exterior. Many believed it was designed to be riot-proof, although Dow claiming the small windows were designed to be energy efficient.

67. A Listful of Dollars

Born in Ann Arbor on August 14, 1962, Jim Buckmaster graduated summa cum laude from Virginia Tech (biochemistry), then entered medical school at the University of Michigan. A year and a half into the program he began having doubts about a medical career, and after successive leaves of absence, he withdrew, having accumulated nearly $100,000 in student loans.

To pay off the loans he began working on computer data entry and eventually moving up to programming, while living in an unheated apartment through an especially cold Ann Arbor winter. He directed web development for online firms, Creditland and Quantum. From 1994 to 95, he built the terabyte-scale, database-driven web interface at ICPSR which provided researchers access the primary data archive for the social sciences.

During the dot-com boom, he followed a job offer to San Francisco, then in late 1999, he posted his résumé on Craigslist.org. Founder Craig Newmark offered him a programmer position, and within a year Buckmaster became president and chief executive of the company.

The 6-foot-7 CEO has been described variously as "anti-establishment, a communist, and a socialistic anarchist," all while overseeing the most-used classifieds in any medium. One of world's most popular websites, Craig's List maintains a non-corporate vibe, and staff of less that 50.

68. Poetry in Motion

Born in Leningrad, USSR, on May 24, 1940, Joseph Aleksandrovich Brodsky was the son of a professional photographer in the Soviet Navy and a professional interpreter. When he was fifteen, Brodsky left school and began writing poetry. In 1964, he was convicted of "social parasitism" and served time at Kresty Detention Center, the Soviet political prison.

Ardis Publishing, based in Ann Arbor, was founded by Carl R. Proffer, professor of Russian Literature at the University of Michigan. Proffer published, in Russian, many works which could not be published in the Soviet Union at that time, including Brodsky's poetry.

He was officially blacklisted by the Leonid Brezhnev regime, and upon exile in 1972, Proffer helped Brodsky obtain a position as poet-in-residence at U-M. He was an inspiring and unorthodox teacher, who combined significant demands on his students, insisting that any person who was serious about poetry should know at least 1,000 lines by heart.

He was promoted to a tenured professorship at the university, and after receiving the Nobel Prize in Literature in 1987, he became the first foreign-born citizen to be appointed Poet Laureate of the United States, serving from 1991 to 1992.

Brodsky followed in the footsteps of an American poet Robert Frost, who had taught at U-M five decades earlier.

69. Greatest 45 Minutes in Sports

At the University of Michigan's Ferry Field, on a sunny, hot afternoon, the twenty-fifth day of May, 1935, during the Big Ten Track and Field Championships, Jesse Owens averaged a world record every 11 minutes. Within a span of 45 minutes, the 21-year-old Ohio State sophomore tied the world record in the 100-yard dash, then set world records in the long jump, the 220-yard dash and the 220 low hurdles. Owens' single-day feat in Ann Arbor has no parallel, not only in track and field, but in any sport. It is considered the greatest single day performance in athletic history.

At the start of the day, Owens didn't know if he could finish even one event. He had injured his lower back falling down a flight of stairs five days earlier while roughhousing with his fraternity brothers and was still hurting as he warmed up. After deliberating with Ohio State track coach Larry Snyder on whether to compete, Owens decided to take it one event at a time.

With each record, the crowd of 5,000 cheered louder. So many fans wanted to congratulate Owens after the meet that he had to leave the locker room through a bathroom window. A plaque commemorating his accomplishment was installed at the southeast corner of Ferry Field.

Humorist Will Rogers observed: "Mr. Owens broke practically all the world records, with the possible exception of horseshoe pitching and flagpole sitting."

70. Polio Shot

During his senior year at the New York University School of Medicine, young Jonas Salk chose a two-month elective in the laboratory of eminent epidemiologist, Dr. Thomas Francis. After graduation, he began his residency at New York's Mount Sinai Hospital with Dr. Francis.

At the end of his residency, Salk joined Francis, who had moved to Ann Arbor after accepting an offer to direct the University of Michigan School of Public Health. The two men worked together on an army-commissioned project at the university to develop a killed-virus influenza vaccine.

With the American public becoming increasingly frightened of the crippling, paralysing polio virus, the University of Pittsburgh hired away Salk to work on a cure at its virology laboratory. Drawing from previous findings of other scientists, Salk discovered a vaccine which would put a stop to the polio epidemic.

On April 12, 1955, Dr. Francis, the monitor of field trial results, declared Salk's vaccine to be safe and effective. The announcement was made at the University of Michigan, and within minutes, news of the event was carried coast to coast by wire services and radio and television newscasts. Church bells began ringing across the country, factories observed moments of silence. The announcement produced a spontaneous national holiday.

71. Breaking Barriers

George H. Jewett II grew up in Ann Arbor, the son of a blacksmith. He attended Pioneer High School where he was the captain of the debate, football and baseball teams. After graduating as the class valedictorian in 1889, he attended the University of Michigan from 1890 to 1893, where he became the first African-American in the school's history to letter in football.

In 1890, Jewett was the starting fullback for a U-M team that went 4-1 and outscored opponents 129-36. In 1892, Jewett was the starting halfback on a Michigan team that beat Amos Alonzo Stagg's University of Chicago team, went 7-5, and scored 298 points. He was the leading rusher, scorer and kicker.

Jewett studied medicine at U-M, but after a dispute with the dean of medicine, he transferred to Northwestern University in 1893 where he received his medical degree. After breaking the racial barrier at Michigan in 1890, Jewett was followed in the Big Ten programs by Fred Patterson at Ohio State University, Preston Eagleson at Indiana University, and then Jewett again at Northwestern. Jewett missed being the first African-American in all of college football by one year. In 1889, William Henry Lewis and William Tecumseh Sherman Jackson played for Amherst.

Jewett went on to practice medicine in the Chicago area.

72. Kennedy's Kids

It was on the steps of the Michigan Union where presidential candidate John F. Kennedy first proposed the Peace Corps, one of his most enduring legacies. A bronze plaque now marks the spot.

The Democratic nominee for president and his staff landed at Willow Run Airport. Senator Kennedy's motorcade rolled into Ann Arbor very early on the morning of Friday, October 14, 1960, with the election just three and a half weeks away. A few hours earlier, in New York, Kennedy had faced Vice President Richard M. Nixon, his Republican opponent, in the third of their four nationally televised debates.

Kennedy had not planned to speak, but the presence of 5,000 students who had been waiting for hours compelled him to address the crowd. His remarks included a call for college graduates to assist social and economic development outside the United States. (Nixon claimed the program would be nothing but a haven for draft dodgers).

President Kennedy felt a special bond with Peace Corps volunteers, and during his presidency he welcomed them to the White House at every opportunity. They came to be known fondly as "Kennedy's kids."

Since 1961, over 200,000 Americans have joined the Peace Corps, serving in 139 countries. The University of Michigan has provided one of the largest numbers of volunteers, boasting 2,235 alumni in service over the program's history.

73. Unrepentant Englishman

Born in York, England, on February 21, 1907, Wystan Hugh Auden was a brilliant poet who made his reputation while still at Oxford in the 1920s, and by the time he left England to avoid World War II, he was considered by many to be the spokes-poet of a generation.

Once in America, he taught in the University of Michigan English Department and became an American citizen in the old Washtenaw County Courthouse. He had an office in Angell Hall, with an announcement on the door: "I inhabit this hole from two to four on Thursdays." His class met in Angell 2215.

By coincidence, Auden's first Ann Arbor home, at 1223 Pontiac Trail, was built on the foundation of the house in which Robert Frost had lived during his residency at Michigan. The original house had been moved to the Henry Ford Museum (see **Poetic License**, page 7). He was openly gay, and the neighborhood children sometimes tried to spy through the porch windows and back door, hoping to catch Auden and his friends dressing up in women's clothes. It was said that Auden was quite amused by their fascination.

Critics and scholars consider W. H. Auden one of the 20th century's great poets. One of his poems, "Funeral Blues," commonly known by its opening words, "Stop all the clocks," was recited in the 1994 British romantic comedy, *Four Weddings and a Funeral*.

74. Road to Utopia

The grandson of the lawyer who made a fortune as the first president of Ford Motor Company, Harold Gray was an idealist and economic dreamer who decided to use his inheritance for a utopian experiment in alternative farming and cooperative living, ideas he formed while studying economics at Harvard and as a missionary in China. After a year of searching, he found an abandoned 596-acre farm just outside of Ann Arbor, the setting for his experimental farm.

Its name derived from the nearby river and valley, Saline Valley Farms attracted struggling families during the years of the Great Depression. George Brigham, professor of architecture at the University of Michigan, designed houses for over one hundred members and their families who worked cooperatively to operate a dairy, orchards, poultry house, and gardens at the site. Members developed a retail store at the farm in order to sell to the public; delivery vans distributed fresh produce and canned goods to Detroit and suburbs.

Canning stopped during World War II when rationing made it impossible to guarantee orders. Saline Valley Farms became a shadow of its former self, and in 1953 Gray decided his once-promising experiment had come to an end. After selling the farm equipment, he continued to live in one of the Brigham-designed homes until his death in 1972.

75. "Crazylegs"

Born in Wausau, Wisconsin, on June 17, 1923, Elroy Hirsch began his football career at Wausau High School under legendary coach Win Brockmeyer. He played his first college season with the University of Wisconsin Badgers in 1942, where he earned the nickname, "Crazy Legs." When running downfield, his muscular legs seemed to gyrate in six different directions at once.

The following year, Hirsch was assigned to Ann Arbor for military training in United States Marine Corps and was permitted to compete for the University of Michigan. He played two intercollegiate seasons at U-M, where he has the distinction of being the only athlete at the school to letter in four sports (football, basketball, track, and baseball) in a single year.

It was at Michigan in 1944 that Hirsch turned in one of his greatest athletic achievements. Participating in the Big Ten Outdoor Track Championships at Illinois, he broad jumped 22-5 ¾ inches. He then left the track meet and, after a car trip of 150 miles to Bloomington, Indiana, he pitched the second game of a baseball doubleheader (tossing a four-hitter in a 12-1 win).

Following the war, he was named MVP of the 1946 College All-Star Game and went on to embark on a storied professional career with the Los Angeles Rams. After retiring from football, Hirsch had a brief career in the movies. In 1953, he played himself in *Crazylegs, All American*.

76. Economic MVP

Born in Ann Arbor on December 24, 1958, Gene B. Sperling attended the alternative Community High School (see **Commie High**, page 46), received a B.A. in political science from the University of Minnesota, a J.D. from Yale Law School, then attended the Wharton School at the University of Pennsylvania.

Sperling served on the Clinton-Gore 1992 presidential campaign as an architect of the economic plans. He was known for his long hours, passionate commitment to his work, and detailed knowledge of economic policy. From 1992 to 1996, he served as deputy director of the National Economic Council while the Council was directed by Robert Rubin, who was promoted to Treasury Secretary. From 1996 to 2000, he was National Economic Adviser to President Clinton and director of the National Economic Council.

As Director of the NEC, Sperling was responsible for coordinating the economic cabinet member's recommendations to the president on domestic and international economic issues. He coordinated the President's Social Security and deficit reduction efforts, and played a key role in such initiatives as the 1993 Deficit Reduction Act, the expansion of the Earned Income Tax Credit, and securing debt relief for poor countries. Bill Clinton called Sperling "the MVP" of his economic team. He later consulted for the television series *The West Wing*.

77. Bump and Grind

Born in Detroit on January 30, 1925, Chalmers W. "Bump" Elliott grew up in Bloomington, Illinois, enlisted in the United States Marine Corps as a senior in high school and was assigned to the V-12 Navy College Training Program at Purdue University. He played in the first six games of the 1944 football season for Purdue before being transferred by the Marine Corps.

After being discharged from the military, he enrolled at the University of Michigan in 1946 and signed up for the football team, joining his brother Pete who played quarterback. In 1947, he played for an undefeated and untied Michigan football team known as the "Mad Magicians" (see **Mad Magician**, page 95), led the Big Nine Conference in scoring, won the Chicago Tribune Silver Football trophy as the Most Valuable Player in the Conference, and was selected as an All-American by the Football Coaches Association. Michigan head coach Fritz Crisler (see **Wings Over Ann Arbor**, page 39) called Elliott the greatest right halfback he had ever seen.

After graduating from Michigan in 1948, Elliott spent ten years as an assistant football coach at Oregon State, Iowa, and Michigan. He was appointed as Michigan's head football coach in 1959 and held that position until 1968, leading the team to a Big Ten Conference championship and Rose Bowl victory in the 1964 season.

78. How to Get Rich

Preston Robert Tisch was born in the Bensonhurst section of Brooklyn on April 29, 1926, to Russian immigrant parents who owned a garment-manufacturing business and two summer camps in New Jersey. As teenagers, Bob and his brother Larry worked at the camps.

Bob attended Bucknell University before entering the Army in 1944. After military service in World War II, he enrolled at the University of Michigan, where he earned a B.A. degree in economics in 1948. One of the ways he helped put himself through school was by selling U-M souvenirs at Michigan Stadium (see **The Big House**, page 20). His keychains sold for a dime or two for 15 cents.

Fresh out of college, the Tisch brothers acquired a small resort in Lakewood, New Jersey, with the help of their parents. With profits from the venture, they began investing in small hotels in Atlantic City, then taking positions in Manhattan hotels. They typically found unprofitable properties, made improvements and raised rates. In 1960, the brothers gained control of Loew's chain of movie theaters. They began closing and demolishing the old theaters and selling the vacant lots to developers, on the way to building a multibillion-dollar business empire.

Tisch made substantial donations to his alma mater, leading the university to name the building that houses the university's history department after him.

79. Abstract Expressionism

Born in Warren, Minnesota, on January 29, 1914, Gerome Kamrowski was the youngest of the eleven children of Felix and Mary Kamrowski, who ran a bakery. At the age of 19 he entered the St. Paul School of Art in Minneapolis, where he studied for three years.

In the late 1930s and early 1940s, Kamrowski lived in New York City where he collaborated with emerging surrealists, including William Baziotes, Robert Motherwell, Jackson Pollock and Roberto Matta. Called the "Uptown Group," they formed the vanguard for an abstract surrealism movement that would over time prove to be the beginnings of abstract expressionism.

Kamrowski was one of the few American artists to be included in Peggy Guggenheim's Art of This Century Gallery in 1943, yet he chose a career of teaching as a way to propagate his artwork, and in 1946 he moved to Ann Arbor to teach at the University of Michigan. Kamrowski taught several new generations of painters, and continued to work on his own projects as well out of a converted barn studio on the outskirts of Ann Arbor. Very few of his students realized that their teacher was one of the most important artists in America.

When asked about his move to Ann Arbor, Kamrowski explained, "If I'd stayed in New York, I'd be very rich or I'd be dead. I've outlived most of my contemporaries."

80. Search Page

Born in Lansing, Michigan, on March 26, 1973, Lawrence Edward Page is the son of Dr. Carl Victor Page, former professor of computer science and artificial intelligence at Michigan State University, and Gloria Page, who also taught computer programming. Larry's love of computers began at age six.

While following in his parents' footsteps in academics, he attended the University of Michigan, where he earned a bachelor's degree in engineering, with a concentration on computer engineering. During his time in Ann Arbor, Larry built a programmable plotter and inkjet printer out of Lego bricks and was a member of the solar car team, reflecting his interest in sustainable transportation technology.

He entered Stanford University for graduate studies in computer science, where he first undertook the project of analyzing patterns of linkage among different sites on the World Wide Web and where he met fellow computer science graduate student Sergey Brin and recruited him to join his research project.

They registered the domain name google.com in 1997, derived from the term "googol," the very large number written as a one followed by 100 zeros, an expression of the vast universe of data the Google search engine was designed to explore.

In 2006, Google established headquarters for its AdWords division in Ann Arbor.

81. Strokes of Genius

Born in Ann Arbor on August 14, 1951, Benjamin Donald McCready is the godson of legendary University of Michigan player and coach Bennie Oosterbaan (see **Never on Sunday**, page 25). He began painting as a young boy, learning from his parents, who were both local artists. His first portraits were for friends and family, but it was not until 1985, when he placed a quarter-page ad in *Connoisseur* magazine, that he was able to make a living at it. His first commission was from the wife of John T. Dorrance Jr., the Campbell Soup heir, who wanted a portrait of her husband.

Over the next 25 years he has painted more than 600 commissioned portraits, using photographs as the basis of the works, since most of his clients don't have the time for sittings. Notable subjects have included President Gerald R. Ford, President Ronald W. Reagan, President George H. W. Bush, President Jimmy Carter, Robert Redford, Mr. and Mrs. Kirk Douglas, Wayne Gretzky, U.S. Senate Majority Leader Howard Baker, and University of Michigan President Harlan Hatcher. His portraits are part of more than 500 collections, both private and public, in more than 40 states and in 16 countries around the world.

McCready is married to Anne Gray, a game designer who has worked as an editor for the Dungeons & Dragons franchise.

82. The Wright Stuff

Ann Arbor's most architecturally significant residence sits at the end of Orchard Hills Drive, off Geddes Road, not far from the Nichols Arboretum. Designed by legendary architect Frank Lloyd Wright in 1951, and completed by local contractor Erwin Niethammer just before Christmas of 1952, the 2,000-square-foot, one-story home was commissioned by William Palmer, professor of economics at the University of Michigan, and his wife Mary, a graduate of U-M's music school.

Some architectural historians consider the "Usonian style" dwelling to be one of Wright's late masterpieces and one of the best in his series based on a module that is either an equilateral triangle or a parallelogram.

Rooms in the Palmer House are small and hallways are only wide enough for one person, in keeping with Wright's belief that families should spend time together in the shared spaces of the home. It's an example of his organic philosophy in which all parts are related to the whole and are linked to the environment in an adaptation of form to nature, incorporating the natural landscape of their surroundings.

Wright stayed overnight with the Palmers in 1958. Invited by the U-M architecture students to give a lecture, he agreed on the condition that he would talk only to them and not to their professors.

83. Running on Empty

Born in Livingston County, Michigan, on April 19, 1876, Halstead Harley Seeley attended Michigan State Normal College in Ypsilanti, and graduated from the University of Michigan in 1899.

In 1900, he met the inventor of a gasoline firepot, the basic principle for blow torches, producing brighter illumination than the kerosene lamps of the day. Seeley and his two brothers, Dana E. and Roy R. Seeley, established the Superior Manufacturing Company in Ann Arbor to manufacture the lamps for street lighting. The business flourished, and in 1911 the firm began production of improved car windshields. Early windshields were strapped to front fenders, and Superior was the first to alter the design so windshields could be bolted directly to cowls.

In 1919, U-M engineering professor Horace W. King approached Seeley with a hydraulic level indicator for power reservoirs, the first dashboard fuel supply gauge. The two men formed the King-Seeley Corporation and began production of the gauge in 1922. In 1925, they purchased the Ann Arbor facilities of Motor Products, adding other dashboard instruments to production. Within three years they moved into a former tannery on Second Street, then to a 5-story factory on First Street. The company had $10 million in sales and plants across the country and abroad by 1967 when it was sold and split up.

84. Twinkle in Finkel's Eye

Before receiving an architecture degree from Cooper Union in 1913, Maurice Herman Finkel was involved with Yiddish theater in New York City where he became friends with distinguished actors Paul Muni and Paul Robeson.

His architecture career in Michigan began in 1915 and his Detroit-based firm designed over 200 structures, from apartment buildings and homes to a variety of commercial and entertainment buildings, including four theaters. He designed two theaters in Detroit, the 1,100 seat Littman-Peoples Theater in 1927 and the 1,800 seat Tuxedo Theater in 1927. His most spectacular theater is the 1,700 seat Michigan Theater in Ann Arbor, commissioned by local businessman Angelo Poulos and opened on January 5, 1928. Finkel's 1,710-seat theater displays a mixture of styles – classical, medieval, Romanesque – striving for compatibility with U-M academic buildings and fraternities.

The theater opened with a live show, *The Dizzy Blondes Dance Revue* and a feature film, *A Hero for a Night*.

A highlight in Michigan Theater history was the 1949 world premiere of *It Happens Every Spring*, starring Ray Milland and Jean Peters, based on a story by U-M vice-president emeritus Shirley Smith.

85. Performing Arts

Established in 1965, the Ark is North America's oldest continuing non-profit acoustic music club. Thousands who performed at the Ark include Joan Baez, Arlo Guthrie, Dan Bern, Don McLean, Karla Bonoff, Laura Nyro, Madeleine Peyroux, Marianne Faithful, Norah Jones, Odetta, Patti Smith, Suzanne Vega, Todd Rundgren, and Wynton Marsalis.

Opened in 1972, the Blind Pig (a slang term for police who were bribed to ignore illegal speakeasies) has been a local venue for rock, hip hop, and electronic music. It's known for early performances by the Dave Matthews Band, Nirvana, Bo Diddley and George Thorogood.

Mainstreet Comedy Showcase (now Ann Arbor Comedy Showcase) opened on November 1, 1984, originally above the Heidelberg Restaurant on Main Street. Comedians who have performed at the club include Jon Stewart, Rosie O'Donnell, Tim Allen, Drew Carey, Tommy Chong, Louis Black, Richard Belzer, Norm MacDonald, Kevin Nealon, Ellen DeGeneres, Paula Poundstone, Father Guido Sarducci, and Soupy Sales. In the mid-1980s, actress Lucy Liu (*Charlie's Angels*, *Kill Bill* and *Kung Fu Panda*) worked as a waitress at the club during her senior year at U-M, where she graduated with a Bachelor of Science degree in Asian Languages and Cultures.

86. The Earls of Sandwich

The brainstorm of Ari Weinzweig and Paul Saginaw, who met in the late 1970s while both were employed at a local restaurant called Maude's, Zingerman's is one of the most successful business enterprises in Ann Arbor history.

Weinzweig, a native of Chicago, worked as a dishwasher (after having earned his bachelor's degree in Russian History from the University of Michigan), while Saginaw, from Detroit, worked as Maude's manager. In 1982, the pair secured a $20,000 bank loan to open a delicatessen in an old brick building on Detroit Street. Zingerman's (its name was an invention – there was no real "Zingerman") sold an estimated 2,000 sandwiches in its first year in business.

By the end of its first decade, Zingerman's had grown into a $5 million business with more than 100 employees, and the original outlet was expanded to a house next door, which had more seating for customers, a coffee bar, desserts, and some packaged foods.

In 1988, the original partners founded Food Gatherers, not just Michigan's first food-rescue program but the first organization of its kind to be founded by a for-profit business. Zingerman's contributes at least 10 percent of the previous year's net operating profit to philanthropy, an effort that has been called "culinary socialism" and "utopian capitalism."

87. Double Trouble

Born in Ann Arbor on October 2, 1989, identical twin sisters Karissa and Kristina Shannon grew up in Clearwater, Florida. They worked at WingHouse Bar & Grill locations in Largo and St. Petersburg as scantily dressed "WingHouse Girls," serving chicken wings and beer.

The twins were arrested on January 10, 2008, in St. Petersburg, Florida, and charged with felony aggravated battery after they allegedly beat-up one of their WingHouse co-workers with a beer bottle. It was Karissa's second battery charge. A year earlier she was arrested on misdemeanor battery charges for allegedly for beating up her sister.

In August of 2008, the twins flew out to California for a photo shoot after being chosen as finalists in *Playboy's* 55th Playmate Search. During the trip, they caught the attention of Hugh Hefner and began dating the 83-year-old publisher, eventually moving into the *Playboy* mansion. The Shannons appeared as Miss July and Miss August 2009 in the double "summer issue" of *Playboy*, incorporating July and August in a single edition. By early 2010, the twins had moved out of the mansion.

In September of 2010, Karissa made a girl-on-girl sex tape with Heidi Montag and a sex tape with her boyfriend, actor Sam Jones III.

88. National Treasures

Born in Montrose, Colorado, on June 28, 1927, Robert M. Warner earned a bachelor's degree at Muskingum College in 1949 and a Ph.D. in American History in 1958 from the University of Michigan.

In 1974, with the elevation of Gerald Ford (see **The Appointed One**, page 4) to the presidency, his papers were transformed into presidential documents. It was Warner who secured the Ford Presidential Library for the University of Michigan. He chaired the planning committee and later served as secretary of the Gerald R. Ford Foundation.

In 1980, President Jimmy Carter appointed Warner as Director of the National Archives, the depository for the nation's historical documents – everything from the Declaration of Independence to the Nixon tapes. When he started the job, the archives were a division of the General Services Administration, facing severe budget and staffing cuts ordered by political appointees subject to Presidential whims, and morale was low. He turned the institution into an independent federal agency, capable of requesting its own budget from Congress, rather than relying on executive branch decisions.

After leaving the National Archives, Dr. Warner returned to Ann Arbor, where he served as dean of the School of Library Science.

89. Try Harder

Born in Bay City, Michigan, on August 4, 1915, Warren Edward Avis graduated from Bay City Central High School in 1933, and served in the United States Army Air Force during the Second World War. Back in civilian life, he bought a stake in a Ford dealership as a first step in his plan to rent cars at airports.

As a pilot, Avis was continually frustrated with the lack of ground transportation available at airports. Recognizing the same complaint among other air travelers, in 1946 he founded Avis Rent-a-Car (with just three cars) at the Willow Run Airport in Ypsilanti.

He established branch operations across America over the next few years, becoming the second largest car rental company in the country by 1953. An ambitious advertising campaign, adopted in 1962, was anchored by the tag line "We Try Harder," a strategy which positioned Avis as the number two rental car company behind market leader Hertz. Such an honest admission, unheard of at the time, convinced consumers that the underdog had a greater vested interest in good service if it intended not only to stay alive but to thrive in a competitive market. The company flourishes today with 4,200 locations in 160 countries around the world.

Warren Avis died at his home in Ann Arbor on April 24, 2007.

90. The Sacking of a President

Henry Philip Tappan was born in Rhinebeck, New York, on April 18, 1805. He attended Union College and graduated from Auburn Theological Seminary, planning a career in the ministry. He served as pastor of the Congregational Church in Pittsfield, Massachusetts, before joining the faculty of the University of the City of New York (now NYU) as a professor of philosophy.

In 1850, the State of Michigan created the office of President of the University of Michigan. Tappan was unanimously elected by the Board of Regents on August 12, 1852. His starting salary was $1,500 per year.

He was instrumental in fashioning U-M as a prototype for American research universities, and under his leadership, Michigan became the second university in the country (after Harvard) to issue Bachelor of Science degrees. But despite his successes, he was unpopular with a group of newly-elected Regents, many of whom came from rural areas and were without advanced education (only two of the ten members were college graduates). Prohibitionists among them disapproved of Tappan's serving wine at dinner; others resented his aristocratic bearing.

On June 25, 1863, Tappan was forced to resign, despite vigorous public protest. Later President James B. Angell said Tappan was "the largest figure of a man that ever appeared on the Michigan campus. And he was stung to death by gnats!"

91. Say You Want a Revolution

Conceived in Lincoln Park, Michigan, the MC5 (the Motor City 5) developed a loud, energetic style of back-to-basics rock and roll, including elements of garage rock, hard rock, blues-rock, and psychedelic rock. Under the management of John Sinclair (poet, music journalist, and cultural revolutionary) and based in a mansion on Hill Street in Ann Arbor, the group created a proto-punk style of music as a "total assault on the culture." The first MC5 album in 1968 was accompanied by a declaration that Sinclair and the band members had formed the White Panther Party to oppose the U.S. government and support the Black Panther Party.

In 1969, after passing two joints of marijuana to an undercover narcotics officer, Sinclair was sentenced to 10 years in prison (see **High Hopes**, page 57). A 29-month campaign to gain his freedom climaxed with the "John Sinclair Freedom Rally" at U-M's Crisler Arena (see **House That Cazzie Built**, page 30) on December 10, 1971, where John Lennon and Yoko Ono, Stevie Wonder, Allen Ginsberg, Phil Ochs, Bobby Seale and others performed and spoke at the 8-hour long event attended by 15,000 people. Lennon wrote and performed the song, "John Sinclair," later released on his *Some Time in New York City* album.

Three days after the concert, the Michigan Supreme Court released Sinclair, overturned his conviction, and ruled Michigan's marijuana law unconstitutional.

92. Hurry Up

After four single-season stints at Ohio Wesleyan, Nebraska, Kansas, San Jose State, and Stanford, Fielding Harris Yost was hired in 1901 as the head coach for the Michigan Wolverines football team. Yost arrived in Ann Arbor in 1901 and became an instant legend. It took two seasons before an opponent even scored on his Michigan teams.

Yost's teams won four straight national championships from 1901 to 1904 and two more in 1918 and 1923. His first Michigan team in 1901 outscored its opposition by a margin of 550–0 en route to a perfect season and victory in the inaugural Rose Bowl on January 1, 1902, over Stanford, the school Yost had coached the year before.

Before Michigan finally lost a game to Amos Alonzo Stagg's University of Chicago squad at the end of the 1905 season, they had gone 56 straight games without a defeat, the second longest such streak in all of college football history. Yost invented the position of linebacker, co-created the first-ever bowl game, the 1902 Rose Bowl, invented the fieldhouse concept that bears his name, and supervised the building of the first on-campus building dedicated to intramural sports.

Yost was known for admonitions to his players beginning with the words, "hurry up," earning him the nickname, "Hurry Up" Yost.

93. Burns Treatment

Born on July 29, 1953, in Brooklyn, New York, Kenneth Lauren Burns is the older of two sons born to Robert and Lyla (Tupper) Burns. At the time of Ken's birth, Robert Burns was a graduate student studying cultural anthropology at Columbia University. At the age of ten, the family moved to Ann Arbor where his father taught at the University of Michigan.

With a camera purchased for him by his father, Burns made a documentary film as a class project at Pioneer High School. In 1971, Burns entered Hampshire College, in Amherst, Massachusetts. For his senior directing project in film studies, Burns made a documentary about a historical subject in Sturbridge Village, Massachusetts.

At age 22, he formed Florentine Films in his home base of Walpole, New Hampshire. His first successful venture was the award-winning documentary *The Brooklyn Bridge*, which ran on public television in 1981.

He adopted the technique of cutting rapidly from one still picture to another in a fluid, linear fashion. He then pepped up the visuals with "first hand" narration gleaned from contemporary writings and recited by top stage and screen actors.

Burns has gone on to direct and produce some of the most acclaimed historical documentaries ever made.

94. Recipes for Success

Alvin Wood Chase was born in Cayuga County, New York, in 1817. At age eleven his family moved to Buffalo, where he was educated at the local schoolhouse. He left home as a teen-ager, and spent the next twenty-five years peddling household wares and home medical remedies to settlers in Ohio.

Chase dreamed of being a doctor and entered the University of Michigan as a "partialist," his lack of formal education barring him from receiving a medical degree. While taking classes at U-M, he supported his family by selling home medical remedies and household recipes that he had picked up in his travels, starting with a single page of hints and cures. Christian Eberback, Ann Arbor's first druggist, was an early supporter.

In 1864, Chase established a printing house in Ann Arbor, publishing and continually updating *Dr. Chase's Recipes; or Information for Everybody*. Before the advent of modern pharmacology, Chase's books were among the most popular publications of the era, often touted as being second only to the Bible in total sales.

Eventually including information on human health, diet and cooking, animal health and care, and household "how tos," it became an indispensable guide for how to live in America in the last half of the 19th century.

95. Mad Magician

Born in Minneapolis, Minnesota, on October 4, 1927, Daniel Leonard Dworsky was a four-year starter for Fritz Crisler's Michigan Wolverines football teams (see **Wings Over Ann Arbor**, page 39) from 1945 to 1948. At linebacker, he was a key player on the undefeated 1947 and 1948 Michigan football teams that won consecutive national championships. The 1947 team, dubbed the "Mad Magicians," has been called the best team in the history of Michigan football.

After receiving his degree in architecture in 1950, Dworsky moved to Los Angeles where he served as an apprentice with prominent local early modernists William Pereira, Raphael Soriano, and Charles Luckman. In 1953, Dworsky began his own architecture firm in Los Angeles, Dworsky Associates.

Dworsky's first major commission was to design a basketball arena for his alma mater. Built in 1967, Dworsky's design of Crisler Arena (see **The House That Cazzie Built**, page 30) was well-received and was said to demonstrate "his ability to combine majesty of scale with human accessibility."

In 1965, the wooden benches at Michigan Stadium were replaced with blue fiberglass benches. Dworsky designed a yellow "Block M" for the stands on the eastern side of the stadium, just above the tunnel.

96. Roseanne Roseannadanna

Born in Detroit on June 26, 1946, Gilda Radner arrived in Ann Arbor in 1964 as a freshman at the University of Michigan. It was at U-M that Radner began her broadcasting career, reading the weather for the college radio station, WCBN. She would turn the weather report into a comedy routine by making radio static noises to interrupt the forecast.

Gilda also acted in many local stage productions. She had the lead role in the Ann Arbor Civic Theatre's production of *She Stoops to Conquer*, and played sorceress Morgan LeFay in a university production of *Camelot*.

Gilda left Ann Arbor in 1969, just a few credits shy of graduation. She went to Toronto, where she joined the Second City comedy troupe. She worked on *The National Lampoon Radio Hour*, then went to New York to audition for *Saturday Night Live*, the first actor cast for the show. Between 1975 and 1980, she created such characters as Baba Wawa and Roseanne Roseannadanna. She was married to G. E. Smith, a musician who also worked on the show.

She later starred in movies such as *Hanky Panky*, where she met her second husband, Gene Wilder. After experiencing severe fatigue and suffering from pain in her upper legs on the set of *Haunted Honeymoon* in 1985, Gilda was diagnosed with ovarian cancer. She died on May 20, 1989, with Wilder at her side.

97. Notorious Ph.D.

Born in Chicago on May 22, 1942, Theodore John Kaczynski excelled academically from an early age. When he was ten years old, he scored an astonishing 170 on an IQ exam. He was allowed to skip two grades in high school and graduated in 1958 to become a student at Harvard University, majoring in mathematics at the age of 16.

He moved to Ann Arbor where he received a Master's and Ph.D. in mathematics at the University of Michigan. He began doing full time research in the area of complex analysis, specializing in geometric function theory. In 1967, Kaczynski won U-M's Sumner B. Myers Prize, which recognized his dissertation as the school's best in mathematics that year.

He became an assistant professor at the University of California, Berkeley at age 25 but resigned two years later. In 1971, he moved to a remote cabin without electricity or running water, in Lincoln, Montana, where he lived as a recluse. He decided to start a bombing campaign after watching the wilderness around his home being destroyed by development.

From 1978 to 1995, calling himself the "Unibomber," Kaczynski sent 16 bombs to targets including universities and airlines, killing three people and injuring 23. He is currently serving a life sentence without the possibility of parole at a federal supermax prison near Florence, Colorado.

98. "Old 98"

One of the country's greatest athletes of his era, Thomas Dudley Harmon was the University of Michigan's first Heisman Trophy winner in 1940. During his three seasons on the gridiron, Harmon rushed for 2,134 yards, scored 33 touchdowns, kicked the same number of point-after-touchdowns, and booted two field goals for 237 career points. He also threw sixteen touchdown passes.

After a thrilling career as a pilot in WW II (during which he survived two plane crashes and being lost in the jungle), Harmon married pin-up girl Elyse Knox, who once had a leading role with Lon Chaney, Jr. in *The Mummy's Tomb*. They became the parents of actress Kristin Nelson, who at seventeen married recording artist Ricky Nelson, and of actress Kelly Harmon, who was once married to automaker John DeLorean. Their son is actor and former UCLA quarterback Mark Harmon, who is married to actress Pam Dawber. Grandchildren include actress Tracy Nelson and twins Matthew Nelson and Gunnar Nelson, who perform as the rock and country music act Nelson.

From 1946 to 1947, Harmon played football professionally with the Los Angeles Rams, but wartime injuries to his legs limited his effectiveness. He focused his professional career on being a sports broadcaster on radio and television, one of the first athletes to make the transition from player to on-camera talent.

99. The Tombstone House

Anton Eisele learned marble-cutting in his native Germany before immigrating to Ann Arbor. In 1868, he established a local stone-cutting business, supplying both American and Italian marbles and providing the carving for tombstones and other architectural work.

Originally in partnership with his brother John, Anton became prosperous enough to build a stone house at the southeast corner of Catherine and Detroit Streets in 1869. The unusual carved stone lintels above the windows of this house are a clue to the profession of its builder. It remains a testament to the centuries-old art of stone-carving brought to Ann Arbor by Eisele and other Germans.

After Eisele died in 1887, his stepson John Baumgardner continued and expanded the business, building a two-story structure across the street. It also exhibited the fine carving which characterized the family home, but it was demolished in the 1930s and replaced with a gas station (the barn survives today as part of Argiero's Restaurant).

Among the first in Ann Arbor to use electricity, Baumgardner changed the firm's name to the Ann Arbor Electric Granite Works, acclaimed for an "electric polishing machine that gives such a high, mirror-like finish to his work."

100. World News Tonight

Taking classes at night, Lawrence Westin, a tool-and-die maker at AC Spark Plug Company earned a bachelor's degree at the University of Michigan's Flint campus, which eventually landed him a job in management at Ford's plastics plant in Saline. The Westin family moved to Ann Arbor, where his son David graduated from Pioneer High School in 1970.

David received a BA degree with honors and distinction from the University of Michigan and a JD degree, summa cum laude, from the U-M Law School in 1977. After graduation, he served as a law clerk to J. Edward Lumbard of the United States Court of Appeals for the Second Circuit, and later clerked Lewis F. Powell of the Supreme Court of the United States.

In 1978, he began his legal career with Wilmer, Cutler, Pickering, one of Washington, DC's most influential law firms. He rose to partner, then left the firm in 1991 to become general counsel at Capital Cities/ABC. He moved quickly up ABC's corporate ladder, becoming president of production, then president of the ABC Television Network Group. By 1997, he was tapped to lead ABC News.

As president of ABC News, Westin oversees all editorial and business aspects of the News Division, including all ABC News programs on the ABC Television Network and ABC News Radio.

101. God, Family, and Pizza

Thomas Stephen Monaghan was born in Ann Arbor on March 25, 1937, to Francis Monaghan, a truck driver, and Anna (Geddes) Monaghan. When Tom was four years old, his father died, and without the ability to support her family, his mother sent the young boy and his brother James off to a foster home, then to the St. Joseph Orphanage Home for Boys.

Tom Monaghan finished forty-fourth in a class of forty-four at St. Thomas High School in Ann Arbor, and joined the Marines. After a 3-year tour of duty, the Monaghan brothers borrowed $500 to purchase a small pizza store called DomiNick's in Ypsilanti. James soon sold his half of the business to his brother for a 1959 Volkswagen Beetle that had been used as a delivery vehicle.

As sole owner of the company, Tom Monaghan renamed the business Domino's Pizza in 1965. Since the store had little room for sit-down dining, free delivery was the key to success, providing a model for successful national franchising. Ann Arbor franchisee Richard Mueller became vice-president of operations in 1978.

In 1983, Monaghan bought the Detroit Tigers, who won the World Series a year later. In 1998, Monaghan sold Domino's Pizza for a billion dollars, intending to devote the rest of his life and his money to Catholic education, establishing the Ave Maria School of Law in northeastern Ann Arbor in 2000. (The school moved to southwest Florida in 2009).

"Adapt yourselves to the things among which your lot has been cast and love sincerely the fellow creatures with whom destiny has ordained that you shall live."

— Marcus Aurelius

Even if you live in Ann Arbor.

About the Author
Horace Martin Woodhouse is a celebrated traveler, intrepid explorer, professor of cultural archaeology, and dedicated vagabond. As an author he is both a romantic and a cynic whose writings have appeared in books, anthologies, magazines, newspapers, professional journals, and on the Internet. Over the course of his many years of travel, education, adventure and misadventure, Woodhouse has cultivated an intense curiosity about the most interesting people and places in America.

About Curiosity Company
A book publisher without many of the overheads associated with traditional methods, Curiosity Company is prepared to take risks that would probably have other publishers waking up in a cold sweat in the middle of the night. Our goal is to publish works we like, works we believe in, which should be the only reason for anybody to publish anything. Each Curiosity Company book is intended to grab you by the throat, demanding to be read or to pick away at the back of your brain until there is no choice but to go for it. Are you more curious about us? Go to: www.curiositycompany.com

Notes

NOTES

NOTES

Made in the USA
San Bernardino, CA
18 April 2018